THE
POTOMAC
A Nation's River

By Arnout Hyde Jr.
Text by Ken Sullivan

GRAMERCY BOOKS
New York

Contents

This 1999 edition is published by Gramercy Books™,
an imprint of Random House Value Publishing, Inc.,
201 East 50th Street, New York, New York 10022,
by arrangement with Cannon Graphics, Inc.

Gramercy Books™ and colophon are trademarks of
Random House Value Publishing, Inc.

Random House
New York • Toronto • London • Sydney • Auckland
http://www.randomhouse.com/

Printed and bound in Hong Kong

Library of Congress Cataloging–in–Publication Data
Hyde, Arnout, 1957–
    The Potomac : a nation's river / Arnout Hyde, Jr. ; text by Ken
Sullivan.
        p.   cm.
    Originally published: Charleston, WV : Cannon Graphics, c1994.
    ISBN 0-517-19455-4
    1. Potomac River—Description and travel.   2. Potomac River
Valley—Description and travel.   3. Potomac River Pictorial works.
4. Potomac River Valley Pictorial works.   I. Sullivan, Ken.
II. Title.
F187.P8H93   1999
917.52—dc21
                         99-29585
                         CIP

8 7 6 5 4 3 2 1

*Below and facing page —
The Potomac Valley offers its
rewards every season of the
year and in all seasons of life,
these tranquil scenes suggest.*

Preface

The Potomac is history's river, flowing through time as surely as it flows down from the mountains of West Virginia and across the green rolling countryside of Virginia and Maryland. George Washington, John Brown, Thomas Jefferson, Clara Barton and Captain John Smith walked its banks and crossed its waters, and much of the American story was written within its environs.

The Potomac River is likewise very much a part of the late 20th century present. Today the river valley is home to millions, the huge watershed embracing farms, towns, suburbs and cities, and subject to the problems and potential of any complex natural system. To its region, the Potomac is a nurturing mother and a precious resource.

And the Potomac throughout its length is a thing of surpassing beauty.

It adds up to a big assignment, one I undertook with some hesitation. Photographer Arnout Hyde asked me to join his Potomac project after I had contributed an introduction to his earlier book on the New River. That one was easy. The New flows entirely within my native Appalachian Mountains, and I've known the river most of my life; supplying a few hundred words to introduce a marvelous collection of photographs was as pleasant as unveiling the portrait of an old friend. Providing the full text for a new book on the Potomac River looked like something else again.

So it proved to be. Fortunately, I didn't have to start cold. I've known sections of the Potomac since first working summers for college money on the D.C. waterfront and in adjoining areas of Virginia and Maryland. More recently I've had the opportunity to ramble the headwaters in my work as a West Virginia magazine editor. The lower Potomac I've known mostly as vacation country and as an historian.

The book looked like an opportunity to tie it all together. It meant a chance to follow the river mile by mile, from the mountains to the bay. The ensuing travel was the greatest burden of the project, as it turned out, and its greatest reward. It left indelible memories: Of a Sunday fishing with my family in Smoke Hole Canyon, far up the rocky South Branch, when suddenly the sound of hymn singing drifted down from a nearby log church; of driving Virginia's Northern Neck in the summer of 1992 in rains so torrential they finally penetrated the floorboards of the car, then enduring record heat in the same area a year later; and of standing awestruck in the Maryland dusk before the engraved names of the thousands of Confederate POW's who died at Point Lookout.

These are powerful memories, reflecting the hold the river and the writing came to have over me. Arnout Hyde has other recollections, just as personal, some of which he shares at the conclusion of my text. We offer this book as a token of our Potomac memories, and as an encouragement for you to make your own.

— Ken Sullivan

Pennsylvania

Maryland

⊙ Cumberland

Berkeley
Springs ⊙

⊙ Westernport   Paw
Paw ⊙

⊙ Antietam

*Jennings Randolph
Lake*

Harpers Ferry

Baltimore

▲ ⊙ Keyser

N. Br. Potomac R.

Romney ⊙

Cacapon River

Shenandoah River

⊙ Point of Rocks

⊙
Fairfax Stone

S.Br. Potomac R

Virginia

Winchester ⊙

C & O Canal
National Historic Park

Potomac River

Petersburg ⊙

West

N. Fork

S. Fork

Leesburg ⊙

Washington D.C.

Arlington ⊙

Alexandria ⊙

Virginia

⊙ Port
Tobacco

Fredericksburg ⊙

Patuxent River

Potomac River

Chesapeake Bay

Rappahannock River

A Map to the
Potomac River

*The Potomac seen
from Prospect Peak,
outside of Berkeley
Springs, West Virginia.
The river forms the
boundary between
West Virginia and
Maryland in this
beautiful valley.*

The Upper Potomacs

Seneca Creek joins the North Fork of the South Branch in front of Seneca Rocks, West Virginia.

Cumberland to Shepherdstown

The Potomac passes through the Queen City of the river,
Cumberland, Maryland, as night gives way to dawn.

Harpers Ferry and Downstream

The Potomac breaks through the mountains below Harpers Ferry.
Thomas Jefferson considered this view worth a trip across the Atlantic.

The River in the City

Evening settles over Washington and the Potomac as viewed from the roof of the Key Bridge Marriott, a scene familiar to diners in the hotel restaurant, aptly named The View. Car lights leave bright trails in this slow-exposure photograph, while a plane out of National Airport creates an arc of light.

The Tidal River

Sunrise greets the end of the long journey of the
Nation's River, as it empties into the Chesapeake Bay.

Evening sun reflects off the beginning South Branch of the Potomac River near Blue Grass, Virginia.

Facing page — Sheep graze in pastureland along the North Fork of the South Branch of the Potomac north of Riverton, West Virginia.

CHAPTER 1

The Upper Potomacs

Think of the upper Potomac as a fan. Moving upstream, the river forks first just below Oldtown, Maryland, then at Moorefield, West Virginia, and finally above Petersburg, West Virginia. The result is a great sprawl of headwaters with a pleasing confusion of names — the North Branch and the South Branch, plus the South Fork of the South Branch and even the North Fork of the South Branch. There is still another by the reckoning of some, the East Branch Potomac, which flows together with Strait Creek in Highland County, Virginia, to form the South Branch proper. These are all robust mountain streams, the main branches amounting to sizable rivers in themselves. Consider them in the plural and call them the Upper Potomacs.

Like any great river the Potomac has a thousand beginnings, in each spring that sends its trickle down the watershed. But officially the river begins at the Fairfax Stone, the original of which was placed at this spot in 1764 precisely because it was the Potomac's head.

This point, the location of "Potomac's first fountain," in the words of British King Charles I, was important because it designated Maryland's western boundary and later the western limit of the Fairfax Estate. This was the greatest of all colonial estates in British North America, the gift of the embattled king to loyal supporters. Its successful exploitation depended upon an accurate survey, and the key to that survey was the Fairfax Stone. Today the marker sits within West Virginia, just south of but still precisely on the line that marks Maryland's western border. At its foot rises the spring that gives birth to the North Branch Potomac, which is recognized as the main stem of the river.

Fairfax Stone, officially designated as the birthplace of the Potomac River, near Thomas, West Virginia.

Facing page — Autumn leaves float on the beginning waters below Fairfax Stone.

From here the Potomac travels more than 350 miles to the Chesapeake Bay, collecting branches, forks, rivers and creeks as it goes. It becomes a world-class waterway, miles wide before it reaches the Chesapeake, but the upper North Branch is a human-scale stream, shallow enough to wade in many places. It has important work to do, nonetheless, marking the boundary between two states and draining a sizable watershed.

The North Branch flows down from the fringes of a mountain vacationland, its uppermost valley running just east of West Virginia ski country and south of the old Maryland mountain resorts that hosted several 19th and early 20th century presidents and countless lesser notables.

The fate of the North Branch proper was less genteel. West Virginia Senator Henry Gassaway Davis, while popularizing nearby Deer Park, Maryland, made it his business to industrialize the North Branch Valley and its immediate environs. This was coal country, and the valley opened a convenient corridor for shipping of the mineral to market along the main line of the Baltimore & Ohio Railway. Coal cars line the railroad sidings in the river bottoms today, as they have for generations.

Industrialization left its mark on the upper valley. Unlike the pristine South Branch and its tributaries, the North Branch country was soiled as factories predating modern environmental regulations pumped out air and water pollution, while countless coal mines seeped acid

Aerial view of Jennings Randolph Dam and Lake, which impounds the North Fork downstream of Kitzmiller, Maryland. The lake employs a unique outlet that taps less acidic strata of water, for improved water quality below the dam.

drainage. Jennings Randolph Dam, impounding the North Fork downstream of Kitzmiller, Maryland, is among the recent attempts to remedy past ills. The lake was built as an acid trap, its day-to-day outflow drawn from different levels to tap less acidic strata and thereby improve water quality downstream.

But this hard-used country is not without charm. Bloomington, Maryland, the next town downstream from the Randolph Dam, has mellowed to pastel hues reminiscent of the Welsh countryside of *How Green Was My Valley.* The people of the North Branch are survivors, hardy folks who have learned to make do in hard times and to relish good times. You will see their

enjoyment of one another in church suppers in places like Luke, Maryland, the town supporting the huge Westvaco paper mill looming nearby. Homes, schools, hospitals, parks, churches and local businesses spill down the mountainside and line the main street of Luke.

The North Branch becomes a stream of great river bends as it grows in size and proceeds downstream, making the Maryland-West Virginia border a crooked line indeed. It takes the first of these turns just above Bloomington, swinging due right, from northeasterly to southeasterly. Soon the Savage River flows in from the Maryland side, then the Potomac eases between Westernport and Piedmont.

Founded in 1888 and situated on the banks of the Potomac River in Luke, Maryland is Westvaco Corporation's first paper mill. The Luke mill manufactures over 1,200 tons of high quality, coated white printing papers each day and is the largest employer in the area with nearly 2,000 employees. (Photo by Lance C. Bell)

Inset — Early employees often donned formal attire when photographs were taken during the papermaking and rewinding operation.

Below — Westvaco's old mill pond served many uses. One of them was to provide ice in the winter to be stored in the ice house for summer use. In this photo Luke mill employees are clearing snow from the ice and getting ready to cut ice to be stored for use. This picture was taken in February 1912.

Industrialization fostered the growth of the upper valley of the North Branch.

These towns are cross-river twins, friendly rivals on the surface but alike in the things that matter. You can buy ice cream at the High's Store in Westernport, then stroll across the metal truss bridge to eat it on the West Virginia side of the river.

A few miles more and then Keyser, the county seat of Mineral County. This West Virginia community is a good-sized river town, surprisingly lively, full of churches and solid turn-of-the-century architecture. Keyser grew up as a railroad center and is named for a railroad man; the pronunciation is the same as for "Kaiser." Potomac State College occupies Keyser's Fort Hill, once a Civil War stronghold.

At Keyser the North Branch abruptly changes directions again, shifting back onto a northeastward tack below Queen's Point. Goats occupy the rocky point, also a favorite with human hikers and novice rock climbers. Magnificent cliffs line the river below Keyser.

Now the North Branch begins its final run toward Cumberland, passing McCoole, Maryland, and eventually Rocket Center, West Virginia. There is a munitions complex at Rocket Center, hence no doubt the name, but mostly this is farming country, flat bottomland given to corn and cattle. The North Branch reverses itself twice in the two big bends at Cumberland, then straightens out for the run to its union with the South Branch at Green Spring.

Patterson Creek, one of the Potomac's many tributaries, flows through beautiful farm country south of Keyser, West Virginia.

Right — Railroad tracks follow the bottom lands along the North Branch between Keyser and Rocket Center, West Virginia.

The South Branch comes off a series of bends of its own here, twisting its final miles through a landscape of farms, fishing camps and vacation homes. Although a smaller stream than the North Branch, the South Branch and its twin tributaries, the North and South Forks, penetrate farther inland, crossing several counties of West Virginia before fingering into Virginia. The country here is pure mountain wonderland, a region of imposing ridges, caves, and towering rock cliffs, all interlaced by the three parallel Potomacs.

The North Branch looking downstream from the bridge between Piedmont and Westernport.

Below — The industrial cross-river towns of Piedmont, West Virginia, and Westernport, Maryland, are separated by the North Branch of the Potomac River.

The Highland Inn, built in 1904 at Monterey, Virginia, near the headwaters of the South Branch. This old inn still offers guests fine food and quaint turn-of-the-century accommodations.

Facing page — A spring gives origin to the South Branch on the Hevener farm.

Below — Aerial view of the Hevener farm at Hightown, Virginia, the birthplace of the South Branch.

The South Branch has its beginnings in well-named Highland County, cool, high maple-syrup country. Highland is Virginia's least populous county, at fewer than 3,000 citizens, and surely one of the Old Dominion's best kept secrets. Potomac headwaters bracket the county seat of Monterey, a courthouse town which modern times have touched only gently. The Hevener farm at nearby Hightown sits precisely on the eastern continental divide, where a single drop of rain on the peak of the barn roof is said to split between the Ohio River headwaters on the west and the Potomac drainage on the east.

The greatest excitement hereabouts came in May 1862 when thousands of soldiers in blue and gray clashed at Sitlington's Hill, leaving hundreds dead on the field and opening Stonewall Jackson's famous Valley Campaign. The running skirmishes carried the Northern and Southern forces down between the South Branch and the South Fork.

Both rocky mountain streams soon tumble across the line into West Virginia, although the notion of such a boundary would have horrified Jackson, his Western Virginia roots notwithstanding. The South Branch, as befits the main stream, preserves a little more dignity and becomes a respectable mountain river as it approaches the town of Franklin. The South Fork is another matter, splashing its swift and boulder-strewn course through a tight mountain valley just one high ridge inside the state line. This is country of almost frightful beauty, the feisty South Fork a kayaker's delight.

The South Branch passes the mouth of Thorn Creek a few miles above Franklin, the creek rushing out to the river through a rocky break in the mountain wall. A water mill has

occupied the site since 1757. McCoy's Mill, the present building, dates back to 1847, with the McCoy name reaching back to 1800, when General William McCoy first acquired the property.

The four-story mill, built to last with its massive timbering and a stone foundation, survived the awful flood of 1985, the worst natural trial since white settlement of the Potomac highlands. Today the barn-red building has been refurbished as a bed and breakfast inn, a place where guests can retreat to a homey room above the water wheel. The current William McCoy lives in town, runs an hospitable household, and edits the weekly *Pendleton Times*. Glen and Iris Hofecker, the hosts at McCoy's Mill today, came to Pendleton with the United Brethern '85 flood relief effort. It was then that they discovered the mill and became innkeepers, although Glen keeps up his trade as a furniture maker specializing in the building of magnificent grandfather clocks.

This is Pendleton County, some of the most splendid terrain in the East. The usual beauty of

West Virginia's Eastern Panhandle — intermittent mountain and valley, forest and farm — is spiced here with towering geologic formations. Seneca Rocks is best known, but there are many such "rocks" in Pendleton, the Eagle Rocks, Champe Rocks and others. They are outcroppings of the Tuscarora Sandstone, an ancient stratum tougher than surrounding stone which stands upright in the formations visible today. Perhaps the most fascinating are the Judy Rocks, outcropping massively at Judy Gap where Judy Run comes down to the North Fork, but continuing in a rocky fin for miles through the Germany Valley.

Pendleton is 698 square miles of sparsely populated countryside, traditionally supporting itself by a well-mixed agriculture supplemented by an old style hunting-and-fishing tourism and jobs in neighboring Virginia. Nowadays the poultry industry is creeping up the valley from its stronghold along the lower South Branch. Recently built chicken houses with their galvanized feed silos identify farms operating under contract to the big

Facing page — McCoy's Mill, dating back to the 1847s, now serves as a bed and breakfast on the South Branch, north of Franklin, West Virginia.

A warm day finds the upper South Branch bordered with summer wild flowers.

Aerial view shows the South Branch as it snakes through the mountains of the Smoke Hole region.

The South Branch has gouged its way through the Smoke Hole over endless ages.

into the Smoke Hole, then a narrow gravel lane carries on for a few miles more. After that the canyon is accessible only to the hiker or paddler, but well worth the trouble.

The South Branch has gouged its way through the Smoke Hole over endless ages of geologic time. The results are spectacular. The river cuts first through a rock notch and then winds for miles among stone palisades that in places drop sheer to the stream edge below. Local people speak of the "Smoke Holes," preferring the plural for the many-faced rocky labyrinth.

Not surprisingly the canyon has made a good refuge, first to Indians, then to descendants of Hessian soldiers who settled here following the Revolution. In more recent times the Smoke Hole offered a haven to moonshiners and others with their own good reasons to sequester themselves. Mostly the rocky gorge has sheltered respectable folk, mountain farmers such as Revolutionary soldier William Eagle, now buried in the shadow of the marvelous rock formation which bears his name.

Remnants of this population linger on, now living within the National Recreation Area maintained by the United States Forest Service. School buses still travel State Route 2 into the Smoke Hole and on up the Forest Service road to North Fork Mountain. The old Smoke Hole post office sat where the USFS road leaves the canyon, at the juncture of the dirt road to Big Bend Campground. A crossroads store occupies the site today. There's a fishing hole nearby and above that stands historic St. George's Episcopal Church, formerly the Old Palestine Church, built around 1850.

poultry companies. There is nothing flashy about the local economy but Pendleton looks after itself, usually having the lowest unemployment rates in West Virginia.

Downstream from the country seat of Franklin, the South Branch passes through a short gorge before traveling on through the broader valley of the Upper Tract area. Then the river dodges leftward into Smoke Hole canyon. The main road, U.S. Route 220, goes its own way here, pursuing gentler terrain to Petersburg and Grant County. A paved byway breaks off to penetrate the first several miles

Top — Eagle Rock, a spectacular rock formation named after Revolutionary soldier William Eagle, stands vigil across the river from his grave.

Above Left — The grave of William Eagle in the Smoke Hole Canyon.

Above Right — Historic St. George's Episcopal Church.

This is a place to spend a Sunday with the family, fishing on the river bank and picnicking on provisions from the store. If you are fortunate you may hear hymns drifting down from the old log church, for parishioners from Moorefield and Romney come out for services from time to time in the summer. These summer visitations are a long-standing tradition, now that St. George's no longer serves a congregation of its own.

For better or worse, the South Branch of the Potomac rejoins civilization when it emerges from the 20-mile Smoke Hole canyon.

Here the river comes back to the roads. The North Fork pours in at this point, well into Grant County and just a few miles above Petersburg, the county seat.

The North Fork Valley is a place all its own, unlike any other in the Potomac country. David Hunter Strother, the 19th century West Virginia writer and artist who worked under the name "Porte Crayon," sought to summarize the place in a single sentence for *Harper's* magazine in 1872: "The North Fork of South Branch rises among the highlands of Pendleton County, and flowing northeastward through a narrow valley between the great Alleghany and North Fork mountains, joins the main river five or six miles above Petersburg."

But Porte Crayon found himself unable to dismiss the North Fork in so few words. "Architect," he wrote, "a summer's study on the North Fork may freshen your fancy, and acquaint you somewhat with the works of the oldest master of your art. Artist, a tour through this wild valley will fill your portfolio with studies worth a tour round the world. Geologist — rejoicing in the abrasions, upheavals, and contortions, the earthquake agonies of Mother Earth — up the North Fork you will find things ripped up to your satisfaction, and perhaps you may find a brass mine. Peddlers of quack medicines and bill-posters, don't go there: the inhabitants are hopelessly healthy, and the rocks infested with rattlesnakes."

The North Fork still takes hold of its visitors, and today it is home to an expanding tourism. The stream begins just shy of the Virginia state line, then flows more or less parallel to the main South Branch. This is West Virginia's highest country, with Spruce Knob, the state's tallest peak, a close neighbor

to the North Fork. The river picks up State Route 28, a major secondary road sweeping across from Pocahontas County, at tiny Cherry Grove. It is a small stream here, nearly dry in the driest season some years, as it travels on to Circleville. This is a picture-postcard town, white-on-white wood frame houses and stores accented by a handsome red-brick schoolhouse.

The North Fork passes onward, past Judy Gap where U.S. 33 crosses Route 28 on its way up through the gap in the Judy Rocks. The next point downriver is Riverton, gateway to secluded Germany Valley. The North Fork receives its major tributary at Mouth of Seneca, where Seneca Creek flows in from the west. Here the Potomac Highlands give West Virginia its best known natural landmark, the magnificent Seneca Rocks which tower 900 feet above the confluence of Seneca Creek and the North Fork.

Seneca Rocks has drawn climbers, hikers and awe-struck sightseers — Porte Crayon "gazed at it for hours" on his visit — for centuries, Smoke Hole Caverns and other nearby caves attract their own visitors, while the river brings in paddlers and fishermen. Altogether, they make the lower North Fork Valley a busy place in the summertime. Apparently they have done so long enough to rename the landscape, the community of Cabins, West Virginia, being just what it says — a cluster of tourist cabins, now mostly new since the 1985 flood but some dating back to earlier times.

The Potomac changes character after the North Fork unites with the South Branch. The river gains in size, splitting to meander around several large islands as it sweeps across Hardy County. The valley broadens, the mountains dropping back to high, solitary ridges shimmering in the distance during the hazy, hot summers.

This is one of the state's few major agricultural districts, and the farming here is chicken farming. Long, low chicken houses nestle in the cornfields. The farmers take their business to Moorefield, the county seat of Hardy County and self-proclaimed "Poultry Capital of West Virginia."

By mid-summer the windows of local stores are painted with cartoon chicken characters announcing Moorefield's annual poultry festival in late July. The town takes itself and its history more seriously at the Hardy County Heritage Weekend each fall, opening its historic residences to visitors in a popular house tour. Moorefield was founded in 1777.

The South Branch collects the South Fork at Moorefield, the latter traveling across town to join the former as it flows along the western city limits. The South Fork was known as the Moorefield River in earlier times, and is still listed that way on some maps and in some guidebooks. South Fork Road, County Route 7, will carry you up the tight and rocky South Fork valley. This area stands in marked contrast to the South Branch country, less prosperous and more scenic, the kind of place you see cows wading in the river.

Top — Snow-covered rhododendron branches grace the banks along the North Fork of the South Branch.

Above — A chilly evening settles over the community of Seneca Rocks.

Facing page — A winter mantle covers Seneca Creek, which joins the North Fork of the South Branch in front of Seneca Rocks.

Nature gets back to business
in the Trough, a canyon
1,500 feet deep.

*Top Left — An eagle's view of the
Trough of the South Branch,
looking north.*

*Top Right — A southern aerial
view of the Trough, which is
north of Moorefield, West Virginia.*

Eventually the South Fork takes you back up into Pendleton and on to the Highland County line. You will pass pre-Revolutionary Fort Seybert, Brandywine, and Sugar Grove. The latter is a trim community of white frame buildings and the site of the U.S. Navy radio listening post. Personnel here are organized into a "ship's company," in standard naval parlance, although as high and dry as any sailors might be.

Below Moorefield the South Branch continues on as a lazy stream in a flat country, easing past cornfields and chicken houses and a popular fishing hole where the Route 28 bridge passes over. Then it meanders around several more of the curious river islands before collecting itself for its passage through the Trough.

Nature gets back to business here. The Trough is one of the principal features of the

South Branch Valley, a canyon 1,500 feet deep running for six miles or so from the railroad bridge below Old Fields to Harmison's Landing on the Hampshire County side. The river runs more or less in a straight line here and one can look well up the Trough from the south end, wondering why the South Branch chose the only two ridges in the vicinity to put itself between. This is float-fishing country, the river offering no difficult rapids and harboring an abundance of smallmouth bass and channel catfish.

Historically the Trough was accessible only by boat and, after the turn of the century, by the Baltimore & Ohio Railroad, which obligingly set fishermen and their gear off at trackside. The modern successor to the B&O, the South Branch Valley Railroad, operated by the state to accomodate the poultry industry, hosts rail excursions on the "Potomac Eagle" each summer. The excursion train, owned by a pair of moonlighting CSX engineers and their

business partners, is well named. Almost every trip passengers on the "Eagle" spot the real thing, one or more of the bald eagles which make the Trough their home.

The South Branch makes its way among farms, fishing camps, and vacation homes below the Trough. The river is wider and slower here, but the valley is narrower. As the river approaches Romney high cliffs arise on the right bank.

Romney, incorporated in 1762, vies with Shepherdstown for the title of oldest municipality in West Virginia. The first settlers, Job and John Pearsall, arrived in 1738 and by 1748 they had been followed by perhaps 200 more; teenaged George Washington was among the town's early visitors. Within a

Below — One young passenger enjoys a snack on the excursion train "Potomac Eagle."

Bottom — The "Potomac Eagle" travels through the Trough, paralleling the South Branch.

Top — View of the curve at the end of the South Branch.

Above — The Jackson brothers display a day's catch of trout from the South Branch of the Potomac in front of the Hermitage Inn, some years ago. Today the Hermitage still serves mountain trout in its resaturant at Petersburg, West Virginia.

Facing page — Sunset closes another day on the lower South Branch.

decade the Pearsall settlement was devastated by an Indian attack led by Delaware Chief Killbuck, the scourge of the Upper Potomacs, and the community later suffered in Lord Dunmore's War, was torn by internal conflict during the Revolution, and changed hands dozens of times during the Civil War. It is a surprising military history for a country town.

The South Branch was settled in the mid-1700's, the years when the American republic was inventing itself. This was the far frontier of the bloody French and Indian War era, and young Colonel George Washington fretted about the safety of citizens at Upper Tract, Romney, and other exposed locations. Ulrich Conrad, the original proprietor at McCoy's Mill at Franklin, supplied provisions during both Lord Dunmore's War and the ensuing Revolution, and manufactured arms at an adjoining foundry.

But the South Branch has a soul deeper than its history, natural qualities that made it as attractive 200 years ago as they do today. "The South Branch of the Potomac is a bountiful stream of water," says Vernon Giffin, who has fished it as man and boy.

"From its headwaters in Pendleton County to its entrance into the main stem of the Potomac River on the Maryland border of Hampshire, the South Branch offers deep holes which the bass, channel catfish, bluegills, eels, carp, and red eye call home. In the shallows and the rapids live the bait fish and small-mouth bass. As day begins to fade into night, deer, raccoons, minks, and sometimes a bear, slip down to drink and feed along its banks."

These natural qualities were as apparent to George Washington, General William McCoy, Chief Killbuck, and William Eagle as they are to modern visitors and residents. They make the South Branch and the best of the rest of the Upper Potomac country special indeed.

The Flood of '85

"Mount St. Helens Without the Burning"

The devasting flood of '85 laid much of the South Branch Valley in ruin, including towns, highways, homes and farmland.
(Photos courtesy West Virginia State Archives)

The trouble started far away, in the Atlantic Ocean and Gulf of Mexico, where the ocean storms of the fall of 1985 brewed with a ferocity greater than usual. By late October they outgrew their watery birthplace and hurled themselves onto the continent.

Ordinarily it wouldn't matter to the people of the Potomac upcountry. The highlands receive their share of weather, including snow and cold in their season and sometimes plenty of both, and long soaking rains in the spring. But the mountains ordinarily shelter them from the high winds and killing rains of coastal storms.

This time was disastrously different. Heavy gray clouds swept inland for days, carrying moisture deep into the mountains and dumping it in previously unrecorded amounts. National Weather Service maps later showed the epicenter of the rains of the first week of November to have been over the West Virginia towns of Petersburg and Franklin. Both are located on the South Branch of the Potomac River, Franklin above the mouth of the incoming North Fork and Petersburg below.

The maps show precipitation tapering off in concentric rings around this storm center, with progressively less rainfall farther down the watershed, a phenomenon later echoed in the flood crest records. The depth gauges told the story: The river which crested at 54 feet at PawPaw on November 5, a full 29 feet above flood stage, crested the following day at 18 feet above flood stage at Shepherdstown and 16 feet above at Harpers Ferry. Petersburg and Franklin are the county seats of Grant and Pendleton, respectively, and these two counties took the worst of it. Ten people died in each. Grant County, population about 10,000, lost 1,475 houses, with hundreds more destroyed in Pendleton. Four people died in neighboring Hardy County and three in Hampshire.

This was very nearly a flash flood, the waters sweeping through with alarming power and speed. A Grant Countian recalled that the South Branch

rose from his ankles to his thighs during the time it took to rescue a dozen chickens from his hen house. The *Wheeling Intelligencer* later reported that Mildred Ernest, the 71-year-old cook at remote Smoke Hole Lodge, escaped the floodwaters by climbing the mountains on foot in the dark. She spent the night of November 4 in a hollow tree.

The Grant County newspaper lost its production equipment and thus for a while the county lost its voice. Editor Bill McCoy kept the *Pendleton Times* in business in Franklin, bucking up his neighbors' spirits with occasional reminders of who they were and where they came from. "The people of Pendleton are a rugged bunch," declared the November 18 *Times*. "They are not strangers to hardship or frustration or hard work....And their background and heridity will stand them in good stead in the present crisis."

He was right, as it turned out, but the test was a severe one. The people of Pendleton survived and rebuilt, as did their neighbors. Houses and businesses were replaced or repaired, as were roads and bridges and even the South Branch Railroad, whose steel rails had been twisted like garden hose. Mrs. Ernest returned to her job in the Smoke Hole. The river banks and river bottoms are green once more. Although fishermen and canoists will tell you that stream channels have changed, shifting permanently in places, the casual visitor may not notice that the watershed has been ravished within the decade.

But the people of the Upper Potomacs won't forget, for the damage to themselves and their beautiful countryside was too sudden and too great. "The flood tore topsoil off in some areas, rerouted rivers, and left piles of rock on once productive land," Phoebe Heishman of Hardy County reported. "Trees are gone which once lined the Branch and the Fork. The beautiful Trough of the South Branch was described as looking like the area covered by the eruption of Mount St. Helens — without the burning."

The flood caused unprecedented havoc in the Potomac River basin, and much of the neighboring Cheat River basin also suffered catastrophic damage. (Photo: Faith Anne Smith)

Even nine years later much of the South Branch, such as Hopewell Canyon near Cabins, West Virginia, still shows channel changes and other effects of the flood, including fields of boulders deposited by the tremendous force of the water. Whitewater guidebooks detailing rapids and other stream characteristics were made obsolete overnight.

The skyline of Cumberland, Maryland

Facing page — The North Branch meets up with the South Branch between Oldtown, Maryland, and Paw Paw, West Virginia, to form the main Potomac River.

CHAPTER 2

Cumberland to Shepherdstown

Cumberland is the Potomac's second city, historically as important to the upper river as Washington is to the lower. The Maryland city lies at the mouth of Wills Creek, which pours through the rocky Narrows down from the mountains to the north.

Cumberland is an old town, originating as Fort Cumberland in the French and Indian War era. Located on a principal route into the disputed Ohio Valley, Fort Cumberland was garrisoned continuously from 1755 to 1766, longer than any other post of its kind. Fort Cumberland was under the general command of Colonel George Washington until 1758, although Washington considered the place hard to defend and seldom made his headquarters there.

The frontier fort occupied the heights where Wills Creek empties into the North Branch. This is prime real estate in the present city, the site of the handsome 1849 Emmanuel Episcopal Church and the nearby Allegany County Courthouse. Stone markers approximate the boundaries of Fort Cumberland, whose history is interpreted through plaques and selective reconstruction.

Motorists rush by on Interstate 68 with little thought to the old fort grounds looming just to the north, but in fact the road they follow descends directly from earlier thoroughfares which gave the fort its reason for being and the city its existence. The National Road, America's first experiment in federal

Facing page — Aerial view of Cumberland, Maryland, the second largest city on the river and often referred to as the Queen City of the Potomac.

Above left — Emmanuel Episcopal Church, Washington Street Cumberland, features original Tiffany stained glass windows. The church was built in 1849 on the site of Fort Cumberland.

Above right — The Allegany County Courthouse, reflected here in Potomac River waters, occupies the heights at Cumberland.

Left — Early sun reflects off buildings at the pedestrian mall in downtown Cumberland, along Dexter Place.

Below — A feeder dam for the C&O Canal offered Cumberland a pond for skating about 1910. (Courtesy Maryland State Archives)

highway construction, began its long trip westward from Cumberland during the Jefferson Administration. The historic highway more or less followed the course of present U.S. Route 40, but the spirit of the old road is better preserved in the "National Freeway" nickname now attached to parallel I-68. The National Road was all business, more akin in that regard to a modern interstate highway than to easy going U.S. 40, now relegated to Scenic Route status.

So Cumberland is a city of roads, old and new, and of travelers. The National Road was merely the first of its important thoroughfares. The Chesapeake & Ohio Canal arrived in Cumberland in 1850 — and ended there, as it happened, failing in the old dream to provide continuous water transportation from the Chesapeake Bay over the mountains to the Ohio River. The canal's nemesis, the Baltimore & Ohio Railway, snaked up the Potomac to Cumberland in 1842. The modern four-lane expressway which swoops through the historic downtown on an elevated roadway was designated America's newest interstate highway in 1990.

Irish canal and railroad workers made Cumberland home in considerable numbers in earlier times, but the city is not what would be called an ethnic community today. The telephone book lists names predominantly of British and German origin and mostly Protestant churches, including many of the Lutheran denomination. This is a city of red brick and working class neighborhoods, comfortably well-worn.

Mystery novelist and Cumberland native John Douglas, now a newspaperman downriver at Berkeley Springs, makes good fiction of his hometown's recent history, but there is no doubt that changing times have stung Cumberland economically. The city was a major railroad center in the days of steam, when the short service intervals of the temperamental iron horse made Cumberland and many another rail town rich. But the steam locomotives were replaced by diesels in the middle of our century, the newer engines requiring less fuel, less maintainance and no water stops at all. Railroad dollars began to dry up in towns along the main line.

"Mountain Thunder," Western Maryland Scenic Railroad's steam engine, pulls out of the Western Maryland station for an excursion to Frostburg, Maryland.

The loss of railroad business to changing technology has hurt, but Cumberland retains major rail yards and continues to straddle one of America's great railroads. It is not surprising that the city hopes to capitalize on its transportation heritage. The downtown Holiday Inn offers "train view" rooms, ringside seats for rail fans to watch the busy main line below. Excursion trains run from the old Western Maryland depot, restored in grand fashion and a major feature of the downtown. This impressive brick train station serves also as the western visitor center for the C&O Canal National Historic Park.

From there you can walk all the way to the District of Columbia, and generations of canal mules did. The route of the Chesapeake & Ohio Canal has been preserved along its entire 184.5 miles from Cumberland to Georgetown. The towpath, a dusty, plodding mule road in times past, nowadays makes an excellent hiking and biking trail. The canal closely parallels the Potomac, built that way to draw water from the river and to take advantage of the natural

corridor the river's valley opened westward into the mountains.

The canal runs entirely along the Maryland shore. Motorists following river and canal down State Route 51 will find frequent interpretive areas along the way. The complex at Oldtown includes a watered section of the canal — the historic waterway is a grassy ditch along most of its length today — and lock restorations. There is a high-and-dry canal boat to clamber aboard, plus a lock house and convenient parking area.

Oldtown's own history goes back much further than canal days. The place is aptly named, for it is an old town in its own right and named for one still older. It was founded by Colonel Thomas Cresap in 1742. Cresap's settlement occupied the site of a former Shawnee village, the "old town" for which the new was named.

Cresap is one of the distinctive figures of Potomac River history. He came to the extreme

Summer view of
the Potomac River
near Green Springs,
West Virginia.

Right — Fifty cents is
dropped in a tin cup,
allowing a motorist
to cross the private
low water bridge
across the Potomac
near Oldtown.

frontier as an agent and partner in the Ohio Company, influential land speculators who sent him to hold the line against the Indians, the French — even the Pennsylvanians, who had not yet accepted the finality of Maryland's northern border. Known for ruthlessness by white men and red alike, Cresap was characterized in a soldier's journal as "a Rattle Snake Colonel, and a D_ _ _ d Rascal."

No doubt Colonel Cresap's reputation as well as his expropriation of rich bottomlands had much to do with the bitterness between him and the Indians of the region, particularly the Delaware Killbuck. Cresap managed his Indian relations as did many frontiersmen, by a pragmatic combination of hostility and appeasement, showing lavish enough hospitality to the natives in times of peace to earn the name "Big Spoon."

But Killbuck remained his mortal foe in good times and bad. It is said that he sometimes lay in wait for Cresap for days at a time, although both men survived the period of Potomac frontier warfare.

Michael Cresap, who shared his father's feuds and who was accused of atrocities leading to Dunmore's War in 1774, built the solid brick house which stands at Oldtown today. The present community sits a ways off busy Route 51 and has its own modest main street. Just down from the Cresap House is the Oldtown General Store, housed in modern cinderblock but nonetheless a bona fide crossroads emporium offering notions, hardware and groceries in close proximity. You can buy pretzel sticks at four cents apiece, provisions for a picnic, or fishhooks for the river nearby.

A portion of the water filled C&O Canal between Lock 70 and 69, at Oldtown, Maryland.

continued on page 56

The C&O Canal

"From Cumberland to Georgetown"

C&O Canal loading facilities at Hancock, Maryland. (Courtesy Chesapeake & Ohio Canal, National Park Service)

Facing page — Dressed as in C&O Canal times, a crewman poles the Canal Clipper into position to enter Lock 20 at Great Falls.

While the Potomac traverses the major geographic regions of eastern North America, bisecting the coastal plain and the piedmont and probing well into the mountains, only the lower third of the river is navigable. Uninterrupted water travel stops abruptly at the falls. Historically, all goods and passengers had to transfer here from one form of transportation to another if they were to continue inland. It was an expensive inefficiency and the towns of Alexandria, Virginia, and Georgetown, Maryland, predecessors to Washington, D.C., grew up to facilitate business at the jumping-off point.

Potomac region leaders wrestled with the problem from early times, building first the 18th century Patowmack Canal, constructed under the leadership of George Washington and others. Actually an intermittent series of short canals and locks bypassing the worst rapids, the Patowmack Company work proved inadequate to the needs of convenient, continous travel. The grand Chesapeake & Ohio Canal was intended to remedy this deficiency. Its ambitious designers expected eventually to provide unbroken slack-water travel all the way to the Ohio Valley and thus to capture the commerce of a growing western hinterland.

Work began in 1828, with President John Quincy Adams breaking ground on July 4th at Little Falls, a few miles above Georgetown. No doubt his was the easiest shovelful of earth turned on the enormous project, which eventually employed thousands of laborers in builing 74 locks, seven feeder dams, 11 aqueducts, a major tunnel at Paw Paw, and the long trench itself. Canal and river were intimately mated all along the way, the feeder dams diverting river water into the big ditch and the aqueducts carrying the canal and tow path across the Potomac's intervening tributaries.

The canal never reached its western terminus on the Ohio, the more efficient railroad age catching up with it in the upper Potomac Valley. The canal beat the B&O Railway to Harpers Ferry, but just barely,

Autumn leaves grace the dry bed of the C&O Canal at Spring Gap.

Below — Geese find the water-filled section of the canal at Oldtown to their liking.

and the railroad was already well established in Cumberland by the time the canal pushed through to that point in 1850. The competition thereafter was an uneven one, although the canal survived into the 20th century on whatever freight —especially Maryland bituminous coal — the railroad left for it. The canal enjoyed its best years in the 1870's, enduring ruinous Potomac River floods in the 1850's, late 1870's, and afterwards.

Today the Chesapeake & Ohio Canal is administered as a National Historic Park by the National Park Service, running a continuous 184.5 miles from Cumberland to Georgetown entirely on the Maryland side of the river. Most of the canal is a dry gully now, with watered sections primarily on the southern end and at some restored locks. Canal canoeing is popular between Georgetown and Violettes Locks, and mule-drawn canal boats operate in this final stretch. The entire length of the towpath is open to joggers, hikers and cyclists.

The Chesapeake & Ohio found its first historian before it had quite passed into history. George Washington Ward, who published his *Early Development of the Chesapeake and Ohio Canal* in 1899, was bemused by the contrast between the grandeur of the canal-building effort and its anticlimatic outcome. "Such persistence deserved better results," he concluded, and the C&O's railroad-plagued directors surely would have agreed.

Top — A father and son try their luck fishing the section of canal between Lock 69 and 70 at Oldtown.

Above — Evening sun highlights the three-span Conococheaque Aqueduct, which carried the canal across Conococheaque Creek at Williamsport, Maryland.

Coal loading at Cumberland, Maryland, the terminus of the canal. Hauling coal became the mainstay of the canal economy for a rapidly expanding industrial nation. (Courtesy Chesapeake & Ohio Canal, National Park Service)

Above left — Looking down Lock 50, showing intricate stone masonry, with locks 49, 48 and 47 in the background.

Above right — Lock house at Locks 46 and 45 near Clear Springs, Maryland.

Right — A biker prepares to enter the Paw Paw Tunnel, one of the engineering marvels at the C&O Canal. The tunnel, started in 1836 and completed in 1848, is 3,118 feet long.

Below — With the opening of the Paw Paw Tunnel, people posed for this 1848 photograph. (Courtesy Chesapeake & Ohio Canal, National Park Service)

Above — A child walks with mule pulling a canal boat along the C&O towpath. (Courtesy Chesapeake & Ohio Canal, National Park Service)

Today's visitor can ride a canal boat at Great Falls. The C&O Canal National Historical Park offers trips from mid-April to mid-October.

Now the North Branch has nearly run its course. It is still a modest stream compared to the broader river it will become after taking in the South Branch, just downriver at Green Spring, and other tributaries below. A low-water bridge will carry you across the North Branch at Oldtown, if you've got 50 cents for the tin cup of the toll taker. The private bridge, the only one of its kind on the Potomac River, is owned by Frances Walters of the Maryland side. The North Branch runs shallow here, with a good fishing hole just below the sturdy timber toll bridge. A wooded river bank takes you up into West Virginia, where a left turn heads off toward the lower South Branch.

The South Branch has looped its way through a region of farms and vacation homes as it swings eastward to mingle its fresh waters with those of the murkier North Branch. The two unite at a place still identified on some maps as Potomac Forks, just below Green Spring on the West Virginia side. The South Branch is smaller than the North, remaining shallow even in its lower reaches. Here it winds through the dappled shade and sunlight of woods and field, float-fishing country.

Below the forks, the Potomac soon enters another series of great bends. Paw Paw Tunnel of the C&O Canal lops off the northernmost of these, once carrying mules and canal boats through the mountain and nowadays forming a handy 3100-foot shortcut for hikers and bikers. The town of Paw Paw — the name comes from the banana-like native fruit, delicious if caught at peak ripeness but too bitter before and too sweet after that short moment — lies upstream and across the river, in West Virginia.

Downstream from Paw Paw, the Potomac continues through its series of bends. The Cacapon River (pronounced kuh-KAY-pun) enters from the West Virginia side at the town of Great Cacapon. The lower

Top — The Potomac curves through Green Ridge State Park, Maryland.

Bottom — Rocks resembling alligators line the bed of the Cacapon River, which flows into the Potomac at Great Cacapon.

Facing page — Sunrise seen from Sideling Hill Exhibit Center on Interstate 68, looking towards the Potomac River near Hancock, Maryland.

Cacapon is also a float-fishing stream, sliding lazily through its final miles of bends and slackwater pools.

There is no Potomac River bridge at Great Cacapon, but West Virginia Route 9 bridges the Cacapon here. Following the road northward, downstream to the Potomac as it flows at this point, brings one to the Prospect Peak overlook. The place offers a broad overview of the Potomac and Cacapon valleys. The well-named Panoramic Steak House stands just opposite, offering hearty fare to the traveler.

Berkeley Springs lies tucked into the hills to the east of the river. This is a town with a dual identity, first named "Bath" and still officially that as far as the city fathers are concerned, but known by its more common name to the U.S. Postal Service and just about everyone else. Both names derive from the mineral springs which have attracted visitors for centuries. George Washington bathed often enough at the historic spa to have his natural stone tub still preserved. Today the old resort enjoys a modest tourist revival and serves as the county seat of Morgan County, West Virginia. The big U.S. Silica sand mine outside town marks a local industry which for decades has been of more economic importance than the famous healing waters.

Downstream is still north, and the Potomac sweeps up as close at it gets to the Mason-Dixon Line at Hancock, which sits squarely astride Maryland's narrowest point. A big concrete arch bridge conveys the traffic of U.S. Route 522 across the river and into the town. Interstate 68 is born here, diverging westward from I-70, which now makes its own way into Pennsylvania. From here eastward the Potomac travels through orchard lands, with apple and peach blossoms perfuming the air on certain magic nights in the springtime.

Paw Paw is named for the native fruit, delicious if caught at peak ripeness.

While the C&O Canal was entirely a Maryland affair, the B&O Railway took the Virginia (later West Virginia) side of the river as it passed up the Potomac Valley. The railroad crossed the Potomac at Harpers Ferry in the 1830's, left the valley for an alternate route by way of Martinsburg, then rejoined the river downstream from Hancock. It closely paralleled the south shore until a few miles below Cumberland, where it crossed into Maryland.

The interstate highway parallels the river's north bank for several miles from Hancock eastward, but the south shore remains mostly untouched by recent change. Back roads too small for numbers on the West Virginia road map comfortably manage all the traffic there is on this side of the river. They will carry you first to Sleepy Creek. The riverside community is well named. It has the somnolent air of a very old place with its big, two-story farmhouses and Hohn's country store, now abandoned. Sleepy Creek's nearest neighbor is

Cherry Run, a cluster of houses with a convenient boat ramp to the river. After that the Potomac —wide, shallow and smooth along these quiet stretches — slips from Morgan to Berkeley County.

Now the river passes another stronghold of the Indian wars, Fort Frederick on the Maryland side. Built of stone by experienced military engineers in 1756, its imposing ramparts were far superior to the timber stockades which commonly defended the eastern frontier. Frederick was undoubtedly the strongest point on the upper Potomac, usually repelling adversaries by sheer reputation and coming under fire only twice in its history, in fleeting skirmishes in 1756 and 1861. Time has proven no more effective against the massive stone defenses, and Fort Frederick stands today as a popular Maryland state park.

The Potomac loops its way toward Hagerstown, but doesn't quite make it, falling back south at about the point of the massive Interstate 81 bridge. And south-

Top facing page —
Aerial view of the
countryside around the
community of Paw
Paw, West Virginia.

Middle facing page —
The native fruit, Paw
Paw, at peak ripeness.
(Photo courtesy
Stephen Shaluta, Jr.)

Bottom facing page —
Aerial view of the
community of Great
Cacapon, West Virginia,
which borders the
Potomac.

Right — Old dam and
power plant on the
Potomac south of
Hancock, Maryland.

ward the river continues, before switching eastward and westward a half-dozen times on its way down to Shepherdstown. The timeless drama of geology is evident as the Potomac carves its way around the West Virginia's Eastern Panhandle, the story written in every place that patient water has played relentlessly upon hard, stubborn rock. That there is no winner is evidenced in the great bends themselves, the river twisting first one way and then another, as stone triumphs here and water there in endless battle.

Shepherdstown is a historic place, settled about 1730 by Germans who first called it Mechlenburg and nowadays contending in a mostly friendly fashion with Romney for the title of West Virginia's oldest incorporated city. It is a picturesque college town, a place of brick streets and pricey shops. Try the Town Run Deli near the Shepherd College campus for lunch, and the Yellow Brick Bank restaurant for dinner. A towering columnar monument downstream from the Route 34 bridge commemorates the memory of James Rumsey,

Above — Courthouse at Berkeley Springs, West Virginia.

Robin Mazzacane enjoys the famous old baths at Berkeley Springs State Park.

whom locals will tell you was the true inventor of the steamboat, demonstrating his experimental craft here in 1787, a full 20 years before Robert Fulton's *Claremont* splattered its ungainly way along the Hudson.

Somewhere along here the Potomac River plunges from one era of American history into another, exchanging the mountainous terrain of frontier settlement and the Indian Wars for beautiful, brooding Civil War country.

You won't notice the change by watching the river. It passes quietly to the westward of Sharpsburg as it approaches Shepherdstown, and it picks up Antietam Creek just below. But it was here that the South's first major invasion of the North bogged down in the early fall of 1862, bringing Robert E. Lee back to the neighborhood where he had seen the brutal war foreshadowed in John Brown's raid and other catalytic events of 1859.

Above — Golf course at Cacapon State Park, West Virginia, a few miles south of the Potomac.

Aerial view of Fort Frederick, a massive stone fort built in 1756 along the Potomac, now a Maryland state park.

The Potomac at Shepherdstown, West Virginia, with remnants of old bridge piers and a columnar monument honoring James Rumsey, the inventor of the steamboat.

Below — Historic buildings along Shepherdstown's German Street, the community's main street. Shepherdstown, settled about 1730, is now the home of Shepherd College.

Jay Hurley and James Rumsey

"Shepherdstown Steamboat Builders"

Jay Hurley checks blueprints during the construction of Rumseian Experiment, *a half-size replica of James Rumsey's boat.*

If you labor under the common misconception that Robert Fulton of New York State invented the steamboat, the people of Shepherdstown, West Virginia, will be glad to set you straight. They will point out that James Rumsey, with the encouragement of Benjamin Franklin, Thomas Jefferson, George Washington, and others, piloted such a craft on the Potomac River at Shepherdstown in December 1787, 20 years before Fulton's *Claremont* first plied the Hudson.

In fact, they're right. Rumsey did build such a boat, one of a number of experimental craft put forward by competing inventors at the dawn of steam transportation — one of them so successful as to offer scheduled passenger service along a short stretch of the Delaware River throughout the summer of 1790.

But for reasons similar to those which give Henry Ford credit for the automobile and the Wright Brothers credit for the airplane, it is Robert Fulton whose name is recalled by history. Rumsey's steamboat was ahead of its time, incorporating a water tube boiler and operating on a forced-water propulsion system similar in principle to that which propels today's recreational jet skis. Fulton's simple paddlewheel was more practical, given the technology of the day. His boat became a commercial success while Rumsey's did not.

None of that matters a lot to the people of Shepherdstown. They stand solidly with the hometown hero. Citizens erected a handsome monument to James Rumsey in 1915 and on the bicentennial of his 1787 demonstration they engaged in the ultimate tribute to the man, building a working recreation of his steamboat.

The effort was directed by local businessman Jay Hurley, who had been fascinated by the Rumsey story since his Shepherdstown upbringing. Hurley and friends organized the Rumseian Society, whose purpose was to vindicate the memory of James Rumsey by recreating a half-sized working model of his steamboat.

Rumseian Society members brought an impressive array of modern skills to their anachronistic task, from naval architecture to aircraft mechanics. By the mid-1980's volunteers had the project well underway in a Shepherdstown workshop, donating their time and mooching sandwiches from Jay's mother, the Town Run Deli, and anyone else who might care to contribute provisions rather than boat-building labor. They called their vessel the *Rumseian Experiment*.

Hurley's crew finished their boat by 1987, the 200th anniversary of its prototype. The *Rumseian Experiment* was the centerpiece of a town parade which escorted it down to the foot of Princess Street on the banks of the Potomac River, in sight of the James Rumsey Bridge and the Rumsey monument. Society members launched their craft there on September 12.

The *Experiment* floated but it floundered, in nautical parlance, the 20th century version of an 18th century steam-powered water jet refusing to operate. After several attempts to start the engine, Jay Hurley gave up until another day, not failing to put a positive interpretation on his failure to replicate James Rumsey's feat.

"This only goes to show what a truly remarkable genius Rumsey was," he said.

Top — Launching the Rumseian Experiment *by modern means, a truck and boat trailer.*

Left — The Rumseian Experiment *gathers steam to try a run up the Potomac River at Shepherdstown, West Virginia.*

Inset — Steamboat builder Jay Hurley, in period costume.

Beautifully preserved buildings at Harpers Ferry reflect the architecture of past times.

Facing page — A sunrise reflects off the Shenandoah River, which converges with the Potomac at historic Harpers Ferry. The Shenandoah is the largest tributary to the Potomac.

CHAPTER 3 ___ # Harpers Ferry and Downstream

The Potomac unites with the Shenandoah at Harpers Ferry, and here the augmented river slashes a narrow gap through the Blue Ridge Mountains. The historic town lies just at the point of convergence of the two streams. Its view down the rocky water gap is spectacular.

Thomas Jefferson was among those entranced by the sight. "The passage of the Patowmac through the Blue Ridge is perhaps one of the most stupendous scenes in nature," wrote the philosopher president, using the preferred spelling of his day.

"You stand on a very high point of land," he continued. "On your right comes up the Shenandoah, having ranged along the foot of the mountain an hundred miles to seek a vent. On your left approaches the Patowmac in quest of a passage also. In the moment of their junction they rush together against the mountain, rend it asunder and pass off to the sea." Jefferson pronounced the view worth a trip across the Atlantic Ocean.

As might be imagined, Harpers Ferry is a town shaped by its rivers. The relationship has not always been an easy one. The union of the Potomac and Shenandoah provides a strategic location and abundant water power, but these apparent advantages have in fact proved both blessing and curse to the small community wedged between the rivers.

On the positive side, the gap allowing passage of the Potomac through the Blue Ridge has also long served to focus transportation arteries through Harpers Ferry. The canals came early, initially the primitive Patowmack Canal of about 1800, then the grand Chesapeake & Ohio in 1833. The huffing and puffing Baltimore & Ohio Railroad reached Harpers Ferry within

another year, seeking like the canals a passage through the mountains and holding the promise of robust prosperity for every place its shining steel rails touched.

Industry came likewise to this town of two rivers, mighty water-powered factories where the essential techniques of mass production were pioneered long before Henry Ford was born. But nature's favors turned fickle as floods repeatedly raked the site, and Harpers Ferry's strategic location made it as prized a target for Civil War armies as it had previously been for transportation and industrial entrepreneurs. Blood and floodwater have flowed in greater quantities at Harpers Ferry than money ever has.

Gas lights along the streets of Harpers Ferry add an authentic atmosphere to the historic community.

Left — A ghostly illusion created by photographer Stephen Shaluta, Jr. on the old stone steps at Harpers Ferry. Many ghost sightings have been reported in this town with a tumultuous past.

Facing page — Aerial view shows the river bottoms and channels at the convergence of the Shenandoah (left) and Potomac rivers (right), and how the two rivers have shaped the town of Harpers Ferry.

One of the most spectacular views of Harpers Ferry is from Maryland Heights, several miles up the mountain on the Maryland side. This photograph was taken before dawn on a misty summer morning, with the lights still on in the town below. Visitors should check with the National Park Service before hiking to the cliffs overlooking Harpers Ferry for directions and cautions associated with this trail.

The federal armory at Harpers Ferry produced 600,000 muskets, 4,000 pistols and thousands of bayonets between 1798 and 1861. (Photo courtesy National Park Service)

Right — Wax figure of John Brown as he pauses on the gallows steps, before his hanging at Charles Town, West Virginia. Photographed at John Brown Wax Museum, Harpers Ferry.

Below — The arsenal's fire-engine house was known as John Brown's Fort after Brown was besieged and captured there. (Photo courtesy National Park Service)

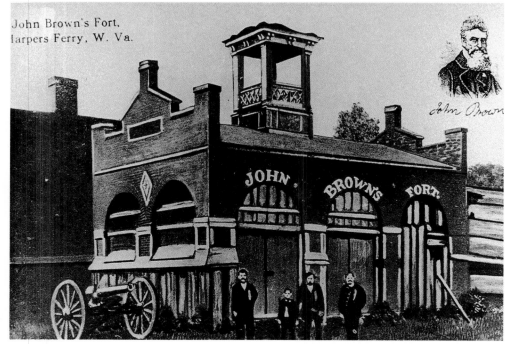

John Brown's Fort, Harpers Ferry, W. Va.

Robert Harper was the man who gave the town its name and among the first to see the potential of the location. Harper, an architect and millwright, was English by birth and an American by choice. He happened upon the ferry in 1747, liked the place, and stayed. He journeyed down to Lord Fairfax's manor at Berryville, solicited a survey of Fairfax's local lands, and eventually acquired title to 125 acres. George Washington, 16 years old and a Fairfax family protege, was among the surveyors sent out.

During his 35 years there Robert Harper built Harpers Ferry's first mill, operated its ferryboats, and built a sizable stone house which still stands today. In 1782 the founder was laid to rest above his town. The times had changed. George Washington had won a revolution and fathered a country since he first left this place, but he had not forgotten the community at the confluence of the Potomac and Shenandoah. In the 1790's, President Washington selected Harpers Ferry as the site of a national armory and arsenal. Other industry followed, great brick and stone foundries, cotton mills, and machine shops, with Harpers Ferry becoming a center of industialism as the 19th century advanced into its traumatic middle years.

The bustling town's importance was apparent to John Brown, among others. Brown's business was to free the slaves, and he saw Harpers Ferry as the key to the South. He arrived on the scene in 1859, planning to seize the government arsenal and rally a slave army around the liberated weapons.

Brown made his move on the night of October 16, slipping over the Potomac from his rented farm in Maryland, and quietly taking control of the sleeping community. His advantage was surprise, and when he lost that matters turned against him. He had brought only a handful of men, and when the hoped-for slave army failed to materialize his militant abolitionists were dislodged within a few days. Leading the troops against them was Colonel Robert E. Lee, whose junior officers included Lieutenant Jeb Stuart. Both wore federal blue in 1859.

Brown's business was
to free the slaves, and he
saw Harpers Ferry as the
key to the South.

*John Brown's Fort in its
present location at
Harpers Ferry. The fort
was moved four times,
being dismantled three.*

John Brown prophesied that the evil of slavery was so great that it would be necessary to purge the nation with blood. That happened soon enough, speeded in its coming by his capture, trial and execution at nearby Charles Town. The Civil War aborted Harpers Ferry's promising start as an industrial center, while ironically elevating its stature in the nation's history.

As the war came relentlessly on, the juxtaposition of railroad, canal, armory and arsenal made the river town an irresistible target. The small federal garrison holding Harpers Ferry at the time of Virginia's secession destroyed the weapons facility before surrendering to Southern forces, and thereafter the place was fought over mostly for its strategic importance on the B&O main line.

Harpers Ferry changed hands several times during the course of the war, most spectacularly in September 1862 when Stonewall Jackson captured nearly 13,000 Union troops there. Jackson had temporarily broken away from General Lee's army, which was just then crossing the Potomac on its way to Antietam, and he rejoined his commander in time for a bloody, bloody day's work at Sharpsburg.

Nature's wrath was the other great factor in Harpers Ferry's economic downfall. Founder Robert Harper felt it first, suffering floods in 1748 and 1753 — the latter called the "Pumpkin Flood" for the pumpkins it carried down from Indian fields upstream. A century later the flood of 1852, unprecedented in its depths and described by a

contemporary newspaper as "an awful calamity," brought a pause to Harpers Ferry's pre-Civil War industrial expansion. Floods came with distressing frequency after the war, the worst of them in 1870, 1877, 1889, 1924 and 1936. Today, water marks on the historic buildings recall the successive inundations, preserved as the proud badges of a tough town's survival.

Nowadays the business of Harpers Ferry is tourism. Even without its rich historical heritage, the town occupies a site of tremendous natural beauty, its brick buildings tumbling down from Bolivar Heights to the point between the Potomac and the Shenandoah. The Appalachian Trail makes its headquarters in Harpers Ferry, and the trail itself threads past Jefferson Rock, by picturesque St. Peter's Roman Catholic Church, and down through the historic district.

Both of the town's rivers attract rafters and canoists. Neither stream offers breathtaking whitewater, but the ruins of industrial dams and other manmade works add to nature's challenges. The catalyst for Harpers Ferry's modern

emergence as a tourism center was the arrival of the National Park Service in 1944 and the subsequent development of Harpers Ferry National Historic Park, but natural attractions add to its popularity.

The Shenandoah is the Potomac's principal tributary, and the river leaves Harpers Ferry much enlarged. Here it leaves West Virginia as well, forming from here on the boundary between Virginia and Maryland. The Potomac broadens as it moves into the lower regions, but it remains a mountain river in the first miles below Harpers Ferry, rapid, wide and boulder-strewn. It is shallow much of the year.

The river breaks through the last of the mountains and into the Piedmont region at Point of Rocks, Maryland, where the Baltimore & Ohio Railway first clattered its way into Potomac Valley in 1832. Here the first automobile bridge above the Washington Beltway crosses the Potomac. It is a sturdy steel truss affair, carrying the traffic of U.S. Route 15 from Maryland into Virginia. The bridge crosses through the

Antietam Creek empties into the Potomac upriver from Harpers Ferry.

Right — Early settlers found numerous rock walls in the Potomac that the American Indians built for fish traps. Most have been removed in the past to make the river navigable. These can be seen only during low water and from above.

Below — One of the numerous rapids below Harpers Ferry.

Facing page — Ledges of Harpers shale, comprised of shales and sandstones, cross the Potomac, creating rapids above Harpers Ferry.

upper end of a long string of river islands, which continue from here down to where the Monocacy River flows in at Spinks Ferry. There the Potomac makes an abrupt westward turn from its southerly course, pointing itself toward Leesburg.

Two dollars and 25 cents will take you and your car across at White's Ferry above Leesburg, a half-dollar if you're walking. A ferry has operated here since 1833, transferring traffic from Virginia over to the Maryland shore and back again. Despite the name, the ferry at White's Ferry is owned by the Brown family and has been since 1946. Their motorized ferry-boat, named the General Jubal A. Early for the Confederate commander who crossed near here after momentarily terrifying Washington in July 1864, steers itself by a sunken cable from one landing to the other. The ferryman will tell you that this is the only ferry still operating on the Potomac River, and it is the only crossing of any sort between Point of Rocks and Washington.

Leesburg gives the appearance of country chic, self-consciously quaint and increasingly expensive as a place to live. Fancy shops see more outlanders than natives, and here pickup trucks give up the hegemony they enjoy in other rural courthouse towns of the Potomac country. But downtown merchants will tell you that they see their share of hard times as they struggle against outlying discount and convenience stores, the giant malls of Northern Virginia, and a new Wal-Mart. Some hope to recoup the loss of small town commerce by luring upscale consumers into Leesburg's historic district, an eight-block area of picture book charm.

The Point of Rocks depot features classic railroad architecture. This Maryland station is still used by commuters.

Below — White's Ferry shuttles passengers and cars across the river near Leesburg, the only remaining ferry to operate on the Potomac.

Facing page — Looking downriver at dawn from the U.S. Route 15 bridge connecting Maryland and Virginia.

Quaint shops along the main street of Leesburg reflect the elegance of a historic Virginia town.

Right — Aerial view of Leesburg, Virginia.

Below — The Louden County courthouse at Leesburg.

The town's earliest history was less polished than its present appearance might suggest. Known first as Georgetown for King George, Leesburg began its days as a rustic staging point for the French and Indian War. In following years it rose to local prominence on the strength of the rich soil of surrounding farms.

Leesburg served briefly as an American capital in exile during the War of 1812, when President James Monroe fled the burning of Washington, carrying with him his cabinet and the Constitution and other precious national documents. The town next surfaced in military affairs during the Civil War, as the site of the battle of Ball's Bluff early in the conflict and later as a place of passage for contending armies. Leesburg, the Louden County seat and headquarters of the Virginia hunt country, is now within the ring of Washington's commuting suburbs.

The countryside takes over again outside Leesburg, a mixture hereabouts of working farms and genteel estates. Proceeding eastward down the River Road on the Maryland side, genuine farm country shades perceptibly into a region of country show places as one approaches Washington. Turf farms growing sod for the suburbs give way to greener horse farms whose turf serves only their own pampered tenants. The residential community surrounding Potomac, Maryland, appears to be as well-off as any place in the nation.

The countryside takes over outside Leesburg, a mixture of working farms and genteel estates.

Children enjoy an autumn day along the Potomac River at Riverbend Park.

Right — Fall foliage graces the banks of the Potomac at Riverbend Park.

Facing page — Great Falls, the largest cataract on the Potomac, is minutes from Washington, D.C.

The eastern fall line intercepts the Potomac at Great Falls, about ten miles above the District of Columbia. Here the river drops abruptly from the rolling hills of the Piedmont to the Atlantic coastal plain, crashing through rocky channels and around the boulders and islands between. This is the Potomac River's most awesome display of power, as the combined waters of the North Branch and the South Branch, the latter's North Fork and South Fork, and the Shenandoah, Cacapon, Monocacy and all other tributaries large and small are compressed down to a fraction of their previous width for an earth-shaking passage over the falls and through Mather Gorge.

Here the Potomac becomes a deadly hazard to those who ignore the posted prohibitions against wading and swimming, as an alarming number do each summer. The falls turn a more hospitable face to the thousands of visitors who cling to the dry land of Great Falls Park on the Virginia shore or the C&O Canal National Historical Park complex on the Maryland side. And Great Falls offers a welcome refuge to wildlife, sheltering a wide variety of animals within the burgeoning metropolitan area. Your patience may be rewarded with a view of a bald eagle.

The falls and the long run of rapids below pose a complete barrier to natural navigation of the Potomac River. Historically, vessels might sail unimpeded from the Chesapeake Bay this far and no farther. The abrupt change in elevation challenged canal builders of the Revolutionary Era and later. George Washington's Patowmack Company solved the problem with a series of five locks on the Virginia side, completed in 1802. The Patowmack Canal locks lie in ruins now, but the later Chesapeake & Ohio lock system on the Maryland side is preserved in good condition by the National Park Service.

Above and bottom — Glen Echo Park was a popular amusement park for almost 100 years. The riverside park is now operated by the National Park Service as an arts and culture facility.

Left — This sheer man-made cut through the rocks at Great Falls Park once held the locks of the Patowmack Canal.

Facing page — One of the many channels that make up Great Falls.

A multi-laned highway bridge sweeps motorists across the Potomac just below Great Falls. This is Interstate 495, also known as the Capital Beltway, metropolitan Washington's busiest thoroughfare. Daily it carries the unceasing traffic of city and suburb in a huge irregular circle around America's power center. The highway crosses the Potomac River here and again miles downstream at Alexandria, Virginia. Everything between the two points is part of the great reserve known as "inside the Beltway," recognized as a special zone by those on both sides of the hectic roadway.

Great Falls seen from Great Falls Park, Virginia.

Below — A kayaker does an "ender" in one of the rapids below Great Falls.

The Military River

"A Ready Avenue for Offense or Defense"

Many Civil War battlefields occupy the Potomac region. General Thomas J. Jackson, memorialized by a heroic statue at Manassas, earned his famous nickname there in 1861. "Look!" cried General Barnard Bee. "There stands Jackson like a stone wall. Rally behind the Virginians!"

A steam gunboat bearing the stars and stripes of the United States lay in the Potomac River offshore of the District of Columbia in the tense time after the Second Battle of Bull Run, ready to evacuate President Abraham Lincoln if Confederate forces made good on their nearby victory and pressed into the Northern capital. It was a fearful moment in the nation's history, but it was not the first time that an American president had looked to the Potomac for an avenue of escape. James Monroe and his government had fled up the valley during the War of 1812, just ahead of British military forces.

Invading armies and beleagured presidents alike viewed the Potomac and its valley as a natural path of least resistance, a ready avenue for offense or defense. It had been recognized as an open corridor into the interior of the continent since colonial times. Barely out of his teenage years, Colonel George Washington tramped the riverbanks regularly during the French and Indian War and accompanied General Braddock up the valley and into the mountains, on his way to the British-American disaster at Fort Duquense in 1755.

A quarter-century later the uniforms had changed, with George Washington now allied with the French and against the British. Enemy vessels prowling the Potomac menaced his own Mount Vernon repeatedly during the Revolution and threatened to divide the rebellious colonies north from south. General Washington came to view his native river as an alarming chink in the national defense as long as an enemy controlled the surrounding seas. He never lived to see the disastrous realization of those fears when the British torched the new federal city bearing his name in 1814, the calamity which put Monroe and his advisors to flight.

The status of the Potomac River was more complicated during the Civil War. The Mason-Dixon Line was the traditional boundary between North and South, but the great arc of the Potomac sprawling just below the line was the actual, practical barrier. During the war it formed a political boundary which the insurgents expected to become a permanent international border, as well as an avenue of travel in its lower stretches and often an obstacle to north-south troop movement. Lincoln called for the extension of the District of Columbia across the river to reclaim its original boundaries on the Virginia side, fretted about keeping the lower

Potomac open to Union forces, and worried about holding the line of the upper Potomac as an intact deterrent to Confederate invasion.

Robert E. Lee brought the latter fears to bloody reality when he swept across the river on the first full-scale Southern invasion of the Northern territory. The rebel commander marshalled his troops at Hagerstown and other points in early September 1862 and then moved toward his fateful encounter with General George McClellan at Antietam Creek.

Neither side won a decisive victory at Antietam, but Lee was obliged to pull back across the Potomac River in less than a fortnight, his invasion plans aborted. His second attempt, halted at Gettysburg the following year, was no more successful and bloodier still. Thererafter the line of the Potomac was never again seriously breached, and Abraham Lincoln rested a little easier in Washington City.

Above — Soldiers bivouacked at Harpers Ferry during the Civil War.

Below — Historic Fort Frederick, preserved as a Maryland state park, testifies to the long standing military importance of the Potomac country. Frederick felt enemy fire in both 1756 and 1861.

American officials of the 18th and 19th centuries faced the possibility of actual invasion via the Potomac River. They planned accordingly, fortifying the riverbanks with shore batteries and larger defensive works. Fort Washington, Maryland, is the best surviving example of this era of Potomac history.

The military ethos continues strong in the lower Potomac region today. No one expects to see enemy flags sailing upriver, as Washington, Monroe and Lincoln feared, but the Potomac approaches to the capital remain of strategic importance, and the military retains footholds gained in times past. Thus it is that some of the country's main military installations line the Potomac, and the banks of George Washington's river still resound with the thud of marching feet.

Washington skyline seen from the Lee Mansion in Arlington National Cemetery.

Facing page — A sea gull perches on a lamppost along the waterfront in Washington, D.C., as if to symbolize the start of the Potomac as a tidal river.

CHAPTER 4 ## The River in the City

The citizens of Great Falls may quibble, but let's suppose that Washington begins right there, at this particular point on what we learned to call the "fall line" in geography class, the geological zone where the continent breaks from the uplands to the eastern coastal plain and where the rivers make their way downward through the resulting rapids. And let's say that the city extends as far downstream as Mount Vernon, Virginia. Great Falls and Mount Vernon are both deep within Greater Washington, in any case, and both had much to do with the location of the national capital.

George Washington's influence in locating the capital near his plantation home was decisive. The first president sought consensus on this as on many other formative decisions of the new government, but it was he who made the final site choice and he who chose the Frenchman L'Enfant to lay out the ambitious city plan.

The original diamond-shaped federal district was wedged between the states of Virginia and Maryland, oriented along a precise north-south axis just slightly off-center of the juncture of the Anacostia and Potomac rivers.

River geography was no less critical a factor in locating the capital city. Like many important cities, Washington lies just below the first rapids of a great river, at the head of navigable waters and thus within reach of the sea. In early times, before air travel or even decent overland roads, that put the District of Columbia in touch with the world.

John and Abigal Adams, the first presidential couple to reign over Washington society and the first to occupy the yet-unfinished White House, grudgingly recognized these advantages while speculating between themselves that New Englanders might have done a better job of building a new city for the new republic.

Both fretted about the problems of carrying on domestic and official life within a major architectural work-in-progress, ranging from the shortage of firewood to the lack of calling bells for the servants, difficulties left largely to Abigal after her arrival in the fall of 1800.

Washington, like any major metropolis, has far bigger problems today, including crime, drugs, and poverty. But none of these alters the fact that it is an attractive city overall and very pleasant indeed in many of its individual locales.

The Potomac lends the city its principal physical feature and contributes much to its livability. From Great Falls downstream the banks of the river are an almost continuous greenway, its major components the George Washington Memorial Parkway on the Virginia shore and Potomac Park, the C&O Canal, and connecting parks on the opposite side. Washingtonians have had the good sense to run their other major parks along waterways as well, particularly including Rock Creek Park and Anacostia Park. Together these bracket the heart of the District, both continuing as suburban parks far into neighboring Maryland.

In a vain attempt to exclude daily commuters, Washington's motor parkways offer strictly limited access and few crossovers. Residents know this and allow for it, but the unsuspecting visitor must sometimes resign himself to an extended tour of the Potomac countryside. As always, it's best to do as the natives do, learn the few exits and the numerous roadside parks and plan forays accordingly.

Consider, for example, the Abner Cloud exit off Canal Road, located on the southbound side but accessible only from the northbound lanes and then only if one knows exactly where to look and when to turn. It is worth the trouble, a restful wayside on a busy road and the location of the 1799 Abner Cloud House and mill site, maintained today by the National Park Service.

Top — Dawn at the U.S. Capitol.

Middle — The Capitol under construction, 1860. (Photo courtesy National Archives)

Bottom — The Capitol seen from a marsh on the Anacostia River, 1882. (Photo courtesy National Archives)

The real attraction at Abner Cloud, however, is prosaic Fletcher's Boat House. Strategically located between the canal and the river, Fletcher's rents rowboats and canoes on both, and bicycles for those who prefer land travel. Comfortably worn, green-roofed sheds house the rental business and a minimal snack bar, with nearby shade and picnic tables, plenty of parking, and excellent river access. Visitors who use Fletcher's as the jumping-off point for a canalside stroll compete with the Washingtonians who regularly jog and bike the towpath. The newcomer quickly learns to watch for faster traffic approaching from behind while avoiding the canal's dark waters on one side and lush banks of poison ivy on the other.

At Chain Bridge Canal Road metamorphoses into the Clara Barton Parkway, a memorial to the famous Civil War nurse and founder of the American Red Cross. The Clara Barton House, Barton's last home and once the Red Cross head-quarters, is located near the parkway at Glen Echo, above the D.C. line in Montgomery County, Maryland. The property is preserved today as a national historic site, a monument to Barton's life and accomplishments.

To generations of Washingtonians, the name Glen Echo was synonymous with matters far less grim than much of Clara Barton's work had to be. The village, which served in the late 1800's as a cultural uplift center of the National Chautaqua Assembly, was later developed into a major amusement park by a Washington streetcar company.

Virginia's answer to the Clara Barton-Canal Road motorway is the longer George Washington Memorial Parkway, running southward from the Beltway's Cabin John Bridge through McLean, Arlington, and Alexandria, all the way to Mount Vernon. The parkway provides a tree-lined passage through the bustling metropolis, with frequent pullovers for parks, historic sites, and marinas and other recreational areas. Beginning on high river bluffs at its northern end, offering views of the rapids below and the prosperous neighborhoods opposite, the parkway works its way down to near river level as it leaves Alexandria.

Canoes may be rented at Fletcher's Boat House for boating on the C&O Canal, which ends in Washington.

Below — A view of the Potomac and Fletcher's Boat House from the George Washington Memorial Parkway.

Arlington National Cemetery, formerly the grounds of Robert E. Lee's estate, is now the resting place of American heroes.

A boater enjoys the Potomac with Arlington National Cemetery in the background.

Right — Autumn foliage frames a few of the 200,000 graves in Arlington National Cemetery.

Below — Arlington House, also known as the Curtis-Lee Mansion, built between 1802 and 1817. For 30 years the Curtis-Lee families resided here. During the Civil War the land around the mansion became a military cemetery.

Facing page — One of the most famous sights in Washington, the reflecting pool with the Washington Monument and the U.S. Capitol in the background.

The parkway is centered by Lady Bird Johnson Park, a fitting landscaped tribute to the former first lady's roadside beautification work. Memorial Bridge makes its Virginia landfall here, a busy traffic circle connecting it to the parkway. Arlington National Cemetery rises behind, formerly the grounds of Robert E. Lee's estate, made into a burial site for Civil War dead and now the resting place of American heroes. The Pentagon is the near neighbor to these somber stone gardens.

Just south, the parkway leaves riverside for a few miles to accomodate the low-lying pennisula of Washington National Airport. National remains one of the country's busiest airports, despite earlier hopes to transfer air traffic to the newer Dulles International farther out in the Virginia countryside. Jetliners use the Potomac as their approach corridor, arriving from upstream and departing downstream. Planes roar by only minutes apart during peak periods.

The George Washington Memorial Parkway becomes North Washington Street in Alexandria. This is the city's main north-south thoroughfare, dividing the fashionable historic section by the river from the sprawling suburb to the west.

The historic area, known as Old Town Alexandria in recent times, has undergone extensive renovation.

Night view of Georgetown and Georgetown University, which is the oldest Jesuit school in America. Gothic spires of Georgetown's older buildings suggest a medieval heritage.

Below — Washington Harbour, a modern riverfront along the Potomac offering restaurants, offices and exclusive shops.

Bottom — The Francis Scott Key Bridge crosses the Potomac just north of Roosevelt Island.

Historic townhouses intermingle with new construction built in the old style, yuppie boutiques and restaurants. Parking is strictly rationed and the occasional blocks of tooth-rattling cobblestone capture the visiting motorist's attention right away. The river front is increasingly monopolized by high-rent commercial developments, but the Potomac remains accessible to the public. A curved wooden boardwalk impounds attractive plantings of aquatic flowers by the Alexandria Schools Rowing Center, with grassy picnic grounds behind.

Here and there Alexandria retains elements of its old working waterfront. Robinson Terminal is an active wharf, a reminder of the day when Alexandria was a busy colonial port, the Virginia rival to Maryland's Georgetown, upstream and across the river. The Potomac River Generating Plant is a reminder of more recent, industrial times. It remains in use, its steam turbines discreetly spinning within blocks of Old Town's best addresses, fueled by the mountains of Appalachian coal piled at the riverfront site.

These places in Alexandria are in character with the unpretentious waterfront visible across the Potomac, a sprawling military complex continuing downstream from the old Washington Navy Yard along the lower Anacostia River. Historically important as a naval center, lower Anacostia and the adjoining Potomac shore today form an interlocking continuum of Navy and Air Force installations. The classic brick edifice of the National War College, standing prominent on the point between the Anacostia and Potomac, makes a handsome counterpoint to the gray, utilitarian landscape below.

Washingtonians use their river intensely. They work and play on its surface and its banks, and throughout the bustling metropolitan area they find quiet spots to fish — by the falls on both sides of the river, opposite Roosevelt Island on the Virginia shore, and within the shadow of official Washington in the District of Columbia. Surely fishing is one of the things that unifies the Potomac watershed. The city fisherman leaning over the rail at Potomac Park pursues his interest as avidly as the sportsman hauling smallmouth bass from the West Virginia headwaters, and it is likely the two would find plenty to talk about.

And of course Washingtonians drink the Potomac and wash themselves in it. Water for the metropolitan water system has been drawn from the river at Great Falls since Civil War times. Work on the aqueduct intake there began in 1853, took ten years to complete, and employed thousands of Irish and German laborers.

They use their river for sightseeing, swimming, and boating. Washington has yacht clubs and public and private marinas for powerboats and sailing boats. Canoes, cabin cruisers, and flat-bottomed aluminum johnboats all share the Washington waterways, and on summer weekends bright sailboats fill the river below Alexandria, where the Potomac first gets it tidal width.

Monuments to Lincoln and Jefferson stand just back from riverside, anchoring Potomac Park. Their modern countrymen seem unawed by the presence of greatness, instead making the park —two parks, actually, West Potomac Park and East Potomac Park, separated by the Tidal Basin — one of the busiest recreation areas in the city. Tourists flock here for the cherry blossoms in April, the trees originally a gift from the people of Japan and now manicured and individually tagged and numbered by the National Park Service. And they come at all seasons of the year to the famous presidential monuments.

Look beyond the visiting tourists and you will see that Greater Washington's increasingly cosmopolitan population is also on display here, Americans of all colors and representing the nations of the world in their ethnic origins.

City fisherman tries his luck on the Potomac, which has become an environmental success story over the recent years. The river in the Washington area supports fish such as largemouth bass, striped bass, shad and white and yellow perch.

Below — Capitol Yacht Club on the Washington Channel.

A five-part monumental aluminum sculpture titled "The Awakening" by J. Seward Johnson, Jr., graces East Potomac Park at Hains Point, with the Potomac and Anacostia rivers in the background. This gigantic sculpture's arm is 17 feet tall, with 70 feet between its head and toes. Since its installation in 1980, this dramatic public art has become a Washington landmark. The piece is currently on loan to the National Park Service.

(Image used by permit of Sculpture Placement, Ltd., Washington, D.C.)

They splash about in paddle boats under the gaze of Thomas Jefferson and play golf on the public course to his south, and they bike, picnic, and fish up and down the park's green pennisula. Mostly, they seem to hang out with each other. Hains Point, opposite the mouth of Anacostia at the south end of East Potomac Park, is especially well populated on long summer evenings. "The Awakening," a statue of a tousled giant seemingly rising from his slumbers under the earth, is a popular attraction at Hains Point, guaranteed to startle those who happen upon it for the first time.

It is a playful reminder that Washington is a city of monuments. George Washington has the biggest and best-known, as befits the city's namesake and the founder of the nation. Lincoln's and Jefferson's are only slightly less popular and perhaps more awe-inspiring, uplifting lofty granite ideals from the Potomac lowlands. Franklin Delano Roosevelt, Andrew Jackson, and Ulysses S. Grant have their own more modest memorials, and even Robert Taft.

Teddy Roosevelt has a Potomac island all to himself. Roosevelt Island, an 88-acre preserve dedicated to the 25th president's conservation ideals, squats midstream, just opposite the mouth of Rock Creek. A 17-foot statue of Roosevelt occupies a circular memorial in the center of the island, surrounded by a moat and four huge stone tablets citing his notions on the subjects of nature, manhood, youth, and government. Visitors who find Roosevelt's pronouncements a bit brisk for modern times may soothe them-selves among the trees, shrubs and wildflowers reflecting a gentler side of the Rough Rider. Roosevelt Island is entered only by footbridge from the Virginia shore, the gleaming *USA Today* building and other commerical towers of Arlington looming over the shoulder as one approaches the pristine glade.

Teddy Roosevelt has a Potomac island all to himself, with a 17-foot statue occupying a circular memorial in the center.

A view of buildings including the USA Today *headquarters from Roosevelt Island.*

Below — Picnickers enjoy the surroundings of the 17-foot bronze statue of Theodore Roosevelt on Roosevelt Island.

Facing page — Fall foliage on Theodore Roosevelt Island, an 88-acre island nature preserve in the Potomac River in the heart of Washington.

Some of Washington's monuments are unintended but nonetheless powerfully apt. The Watergate put a new word into the language, and it will be the next century, if ever, before Americans can pass the ritzy complex without thinking of Richard Nixon. To the city's political aficionados the Reflecting Pool is no less a reminder of once-mighty Congressman Wilbur Mills's drunken late-night dip with an off-duty stripper. The District has its other informal memorials to the best and worst qualities of the people who have governed here for two centuries.

And Washington is a city of bridges, more than a half-dozen sweeping across the Potomac and others spanning the Anacostia and Rock Creek. Most are named for past leaders, Theodore Roosevelt, Frederick Douglass and others, or otherwise connected to Washington's rich history.

The grandest is the Arlington Memorial Bridge, which crosses on a direct and ironic axis from Arlington House, which was Robert E. Lee's mansion, to the Lincoln Memorial. This wide bridge is as much monument as roadway, its approaches guarded by golden horsemen and its stately arches marching triumphantly from the District of Columbia to the Commonwealth of Virginia, spanning in stone what once threatened to widen into an international border. It stands in marked contrast to the utilitarian bridges of more recent origins, symbolized by the Woodrow Wilson Bridge, all concrete piers and practicality as it carries Beltway traffic across the Potomac a few miles downstream.

Top — Golden horsemen adorn Arlington Memorial Bridge, which passes from Washington to Arlington.

Above — Sculling the Potomac with the Arlington Memorial Bridge in the background.

Looking at Washington from the air one sees that the Potomac passes quickly from its falls and rapids to a series of islands and elongated penninsulas, nearly islands themselves. One can imagine the day when Captain John Smith fished here, and the Anacostia Indians reaped an abundant livelihood from these waters and the lush surrounding forests. A fur trader of a few years later described the area as "the most pleasant and healthful place in all this country."

It remains pleasant today, and it is easy to see why our betters get so comfortable here. They come from all over, the politicians, career bureaucrats and consultants who grapple together to run the government but sometimes seem to have so tenuous a grasp on this great country itself. They settle in and are loath to leave, their vision said to be restricted to the confines of the Beltway which circles them.

Many of them crisscross the Potomac daily, and they would do well to follow it into the countryside, upstream or down. They will discover that the tributaries stretch a good way into the interior of the American continent, to a place where folks are as likely to follow the Steelers as the Redskins and where most make their living in ways having little to do with government. The headwaters have been settled since George Washington's day, and the lower river was old country when he was born, so the Potomac may be said probe a long way into the heart of the American people as well. The countryside has changed, but maybe the people haven't, that much. Both merit attention.

The trip is an eye-opener, and a sure cure for Potomac Fever.

Top — The Vietnam Women's Memorial, unveiled on Veterans Day 1993. This realistic sculpture was made possible by the crusading efforts of a former Army nurse, Diane Carlson, and sculpted by Glenna Goodacre. Many mementoes were left at the memorial during Veterans Day weekend.

Below — The United States Marine Corps Memorial, based on the photograph of the raising of the American flag on Iwo Jima February 19, 1945, is one of the capitol area's many monuments.

Modern satellite imaging shows an unusual view of the Potomac basin. Areas may be identified by color variations, the dark gray tones depicting greatest population density or most intense commercial development. The water condition of the Potomac and the Chesapeake Bay may also be detected, the lighter shades of blue showing greater quantities of silt. Such images as this are increasingly used in water quality research and in land use planning. (Courtesy National Aeronautics and Space Administration)

Waves pounding the beach at Point Lookout signal an impending storm.

CHAPTER 5   # The Tidal River

Below the District of Columbia, the Potomac becomes a world-class river, carrying ships, fishing boats, and pleasure craft on its expansive surface and an abundance of aquatic life within its depths as it eases relentlessly to sea level. Majestic now, a broad, slow-moving, tidewater stream, increasingly salty, the Potomac flows down past Mount Vernon, the estate and burial place of the man to whom the river meant a highway into the heart of the continent and an axis around which to build a nation. It flows here through the earliest years of American history, through country first settled by Europeans three and a half centuries ago.

Leaving the District and Mount Vernon behind, the Potomac passes on toward Gunston Hall, the home of George Washington's neighbor and fellow patriot, the independent-minded George Mason. Below Gunston the widening river swings through its Big Bend, a great left

hook coursing first southwesterly then hard eastward and even northerly before dropping south again around Mathias Point.

Riverside military installations confirm the long-standing strategic importance of this area so near the national capital, first Fort Belvoir on the Virginia side, then Indian Head Naval Station in Maryland, and next the huge Marine Corps reservation at Quantico, Virginia. Smaller compounds dot the river from here to the Chesapeake Bay, as do the remains of forts which defended the naval approaches to the District of Columbia in earlier times. Fort Washington is the most significant of the latter, overlooking the Potomac upriver from Mount Vernon on the Maryland shore. This outstanding 19th-century fort was built in 1809, destroyed by the British during the War of 1812, and rebuilt during the 1820's.

94287

Top — Destroyed by friendly fire, these are among the hundreds of unused World War I troopships stripped and burned in the Potomac during 1925. The hulls were towed to Mallows Bay, Maryland, to salvage remaining metal.
(Photo courtesy National Archives)

Above — Aerial view of the Mallows Bay ship graveyard today.

A more curious monument to Potomac military history survives at Mallows Bay, below Quantico on the Maryland side of the river. Here lie the gutted remains of dozens of unused wooden troopships from World War I, built just at the time the United States was first most seriously concerned with projecting its might overseas but nonetheless ironically brought home to rest at Washington's doorstep. The interlocking wrecks lie honeycombed together on the shallow river bottom, rising above the water as the outlines of eerily symmetrical islands now covered with brush and trees.

The Potomac River in its lowest stretches is too wide for bridges. The last one crosses just below Mathias Point, a two-lane toll bridge from Dahlgren, Virginia, to the Maryland shore. The long bridge is named for Maryland Governor Harry Nice, and the toll is collected on the Maryland side, just as it is done far upstream at Whites Ferry and the Oldtown toll bridge.

The domicile of the toll takers is an interesting coincidence reflecting historic fact. Excepting only the few miles within the District of Columbia, the State of Maryland owns the main stem of the Potomac from the highest headwaters of the North Branch to the Chesapeake Bay. The Virginia and West Virginia boundaries hug their respective shores, with the residents of those two states obliged to buy Maryland licenses even to fish the river's waters. Maryland's title dates back to rights granted to Lord Baltimore by King Charles I and later upheld by the United States Supreme Court.

The Nice Memorial Bridge spans nearly two miles of river water, striking land on the Maryland side just above the sprawling Potomac Electric Power Company plant. Put the towering Pepco stacks behind you as you pass into Charles County, tobacco country since colonial days and proud to remain so even in these health-conscious times. Curing barns loom in the fields back from the road, showing broad tin roofs and vertical ventilator slots which pierce the weathered wood barn sides from top to bottom. The smell when the big barns are full of golden burley in the fall is intoxicating.

Gutted remains of unused wooden troopships from World War I are honeycombed together at Mallows Bay.

Mallows Bay shipwrecks which once blazed with all the colors of a giant salvage fire burn here with the cold hues of infrared photography.

Sun and clouds make
a backdrop for the
Nice Memorial Bridge
which crosses the
Potomac between
Charles County, Maryland,
and George County,
Virginia. This bridge
spans almost two miles.

The Potomac Plantations

"Several Homes Survive Today"

A rainbow highlights Mount Vernon, most famous of the Potomac River estates. (Photo courtesy Ted Vaughan, The Mount Vernon Ladies' Association)

The early plantation system reached its full expression in the lower Potomac country, particularly along the Virginia shore. Great farms lined the river and its creeks and tidal inlets, striving grandly and mostly unsuccessfully for economic self-sufficiency. In the meantime, their wharves kept the plantation owners in touch with the world, including exploitative creditors in Britain who took their tobacco, sent them back the luxuries and necessities of the Potomac River good life, and from year to year piled up a growing debt against them. It was a peculiar mix of dependence and self-reliance, and of the ardent desire on the part of the planters to pass wholly from one to the other. Curiously, it bred the founders of American democracy.

Several of their homes survive today. Traveling downriver, the first of these is Arlington House, the Custis-Lee mansion at Arlington National Cemetery in Virginia. This beautiful place was not always a graveyard. Before the Civil War it was the estate of the Custis family, and the home of Robert E. Lee after his marriage to Mary Custis in 1831. From its hillside the mansion overlooks the Potomac River and the city of Washington on the other side. Lee resigned his commission in the U.S. Army here in 1861, and the strategically located property was soon occupied by federal troops. By war's end Arlington had been seized for non-payment of taxes to a government its owners no longer acknowledged.

George Washington also had Custis family connections, marrying in 1759 the wealthy widow Martha Dandridge Custis — the grandmother to Lee's father-in-law, as it happened. Mount Vernon came down to him through his brother Lawrence, however, and Washington himself is responsible for the current shape of the house, redesigning and expanding the original structure several times. The mansion commands broad views of the Potomac, which in times past supplied a good part of the plantation food through its fish and shellfish and provided transportation to neighboring plantations and beyond. Visitors reach Mount Vernon by automobile today, many traveling down the George Washington Memorial Parkway, the pleasant riverside drive which bisects metropolitan Washington on the Virginia side of the Potomac.

Belvoir, the nearby Fairfax family mansion and youthful George Washington's model of the aristocratic life, no longer stands. Today the Fairfax estate is one of the Potomac's ghost plantations, its site occupied by sprawling Fort Belvoir. The house burned during the Revolutionary War, and its remaining ruins were destroyed by invading British troops during the War of 1812. Washington, once a Fairfax protege and a frequent visitor to Belvoir, commented that he had spent "the happiest moments of my life" there and was overcome by sorrow at its loss to fire.

Another Potomac River ghost is Nomini Hall, its Westmoreland County site marked today only by an entry lane of towering tulip poplars. Nomini, which burned in 1850, is remembered as the home of Robert Carter III. Carter's grandfather, the original Robert ("King") Carter, was one of the greatest colonial planters. King Carter had owned most of the Northern Neck in his time, thriving in grand manner under British rule, but his grandson evidently took the libertarian ideals of the later Revolution seriously. Carter the Third freed his 500 slaves beginning in 1791, the largest private emancipation in American history and now an enduring part of Potomac River legend and history.

Gunston Hall is Mount Vernon's nearest surviving plantation neighbor downstream on the Potomac. The brick Georgian mansion was the home of George Mason, Washington's contemporary and the author of essential American civil liberties. The 1755 manor house is open for tours today and nearby grounds form the Mason Neck wildlife preserve.

Still farther downstream, Stratford Hall is the last and arguably the greatest of the surviving Potomac River plantation houses. The red-brick mansion is best known as the birthplace of Robert E. Lee, but Stratford was already generations old by the time of the famous general's birth there in 1807. The house was built by Thomas Lee, Robert's ancestor on his mother's side, in the 1730's. The graceful H-shaped mansion is an outstanding example of Colonial architecture. Today more than 1,600 acres are farmed as a working plantation by the Robert E. Lee Memorial Association.

Above — Silhouette of Mount Vernon, its form shaped by George Washington himself.

Left — Flowers typical of Washington's time flourish amid the grounds of his estate.

Below — Rocking chairs on the porch of Mount Vernon, with the Potomac in the background.

The Potomac plantations welcome visitors. These are not sterile house museums, wrenched out of context as the historic houses of cities sometimes must be. Plantations were the economic as well as social units of their day, working farms and the family homes of rising American dynasties. Mount Vernon, Gunston, and Stratford each make an effort to recreate the plantation as a going concern, with the selective preservation and reconstruction of supporting outbuildings and grounds. Popes Creek Plantation, Stratford's neighbor and Washington's birthplace, is devoted entirely to a recreation of the functional plantation, with no attempt to rebuild the original house.

Collectively, these plantations comprise an impressive slice of our national history. Touring them together, as it is possible to do in a long summer day or two, affords a glimpse into the practical as well as elegant sides of Potomac River society in its heyday.

Right — Gunston Hall as seen through the latticework of one of the gazebos on the grounds of this fine old plantation.

Below — Aerial view of Gunston Hall, the home of George Mason.

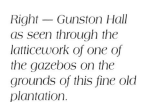

Top Left — Stratford Hall, one of the great houses of American history, was built by Thomas Lee in the late 1720's and early 1730's.

Top right — Grist mill at Stratford Hall, rebuilt on the original foundation.

Right — Dining room at Stratford Hall.

Below — Popes Creek Plantation, George Washington's birthplace on the banks of the Potomac in Westmoreland County, Virginia, has been restored as a working colonial farm.

The Dove, *a floating replica of one of the square-rigged sailing ships which brought Maryland's first settlers in the 1630's, lies at anchor at Historic St. Marys City.*

Tobacco culture in these lower river counties goes back to the first generation of white residents, Virginians as it happened. Captain John Smith is credited as first among Englishmen to explore the Potomac River, venturing out from Jamestown in the summer of 1608, the year after first settlement there. Smith and his men made their way by boat up the Chesapeake and into the Potomac, apparently traveling all the way to the head of navigation at present Washington. They found fish so thick that they tried to catch them with frying pans, Smith reporting that he had seen "neither better fish, more plenty, nor more variety" anywhere else in all his travels.

And John Smith also found people a-plenty on the Potomac ahead of him. The rich riverside lands were thickly populated by native tribes, the lower groups adhering to the powerful Powhatan confederacy. Chief Powhatan's allies already had had their fill of Europeans, and Smith's group found a friendlier reception among rival Indians farther upstream. But wherever the explorers traveled they found the most desirable points — the mouth of Anacostia, Port Tobacco, and other places soon coveted by white immigrants — already settled by their native predecessors. The work of dispossession and displacement soon to begin here was the first installment in a very long chapter of American history.

The original residents of the Potomac basin left their imprint, especially on the cultural landscape. The name Potomac itself is thought to have come from an Indian term meaning something like "trading place," reflecting economic diversity and the prosperity of native inhabitants having a surplus to trade with neighbors near and far. The earliest Europeans readily accomodated themselves to the native economy, buying and selling from the Indians and among themselves, confirming the river's status as an avenue of commerce. These first white men lived lightly on the land and water, trapping and trading and conniving for advantage.

But soon they were followed by more permanent settlers. The first of these were Lord Baltimore's Catholics, who sailed hopefully up the wide river in 1634 in ships named the *Ark* and the *Dove*.

The Catholic immigrants were led by Baltimore's brother, Leonard Calvert, and the Jesuit priest Andrew White, the latter so impressed by the Potomac River that he said the Thames was "but a little finger" compared to it. They founded the colony and future state of Maryland on the river's north shore, establishing their first capital at St. Marys, and by their presence and their own tolerance they helped to lay the foundation of religious freedom in America. Historic St. Marys City is a major land-mark of the Potomac north shore today, featuring the Old State House, a working 17th-century tobacco plantation, and a floating reconstruction of the *Dove* among its attractions.

The south shore was Virginia's own. The pennisula between the Potomac and the Rappahannock rivers is called the Northern Neck. It was among the areas first settled after James-town, and it proved to be a breeding ground for leadership. Here within a few miles of each other in Westmoreland County were born George Washington, James Monroe and Robert E. Lee — as well as Lee's uncles, Richard Henry Lee and Francis Lightfoot Lee, the only brothers to sign the Declaration of Independence. Citing these and others, the Potomac historian Frederick Gutheim concluded a generation ago that the

Historic St. Marys City features a reconstruction of the Dove, one of the ships to bring Maryland's first settlers.

Jack Oblein takes a navigational sighting on the Dove, which makes sailing voyages on the Potomac. Volunteers help work and maintain the ship.

Northern Neck statesmen represented a galaxy of "lawgivers, heroes, philosophers, presidents" whose magnitude "cannot be equaled in any corresponding time and place in our country."

Despite this record at birthing greatness, out-of-the-way Westmoreland failed to reach the material prosperity of other Virginia counties. Its representative to an 1871 statewide industrial convention was not abashed. Called upon to name his county's main products, delegate W. W. Walker acknowledged that Westmoreland did not produce "the fat cattle of Highland, the golden wheat of Augusta, the iron of Bedford, the rich corn of Rockingham," nor the riches of other favored precincts of the Old Dominion. "Mr. Chairman, you have asked me what Westmoreland produces," Walker exclaimed. "I will now answer you. Westmoreland produces men!"

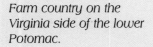

Farm country on the Virginia side of the lower Potomac.

Ironically, it was in this cradle of bold-thinking Virginians that the slavery took root that John Brown would try to undo upriver at Harpers Ferry generations later with such momentous results. For though the Northern Neck's tobbaco lands wore down soon and the area never matched Virginia's more fertile regions in the fruitfulness of its agriculture, its farms and plantations were among the first to depend on slave labor, their bondsmen numbering in the ones and twos, in the dozens, in the scores, and in some few cases in the hundreds.

Dependents of slaves and slaveholders mix freely today, but the lower Potomac country retains its historic character. The Maryland side remains Catholic in flavor, in its place names, its churches and its occasional roadside shrines to the Virgin. Taverns and country roadhouses suggest a relaxed rural lifestyle.

The Virginia shore remains predominantly Protestant, as it was historically. This was a land of great plantations. Stratford Hall, one of the greatest, overlooks the Potomac today as it has for more than 250 years. The Lee family mansion, Stratford survives as one of the remaining architectural treasures from Colonial America and the showplace of the Northern Neck.

The lower Potomac country has not been overrun by tourists despite its proximity to major population centers. This is farming country. The Northern Neck is given over to wheat, corn, and soybeans. At harvest time, big farm machines two lanes wide crowd traffic from major secondary roads as they move from field to field. Residents not busy in the fields may work in pulpwood timbering, or the fishing and marine industries.

Visitors can expect to accomodate themselves to the character of the place, rather than vice versa. Potomac Beach is indicative of the easy-going nature of the area. The Virginia town offers fishing piers with resident ospreys and a distant view of the Pepco plant, a pebbled waterfront, and Wilkerson's, a respected seafood restaurant. Nearby Colonial Beach has its own old pier with restaurant, as well as an inviting modern chain motel at river's edge. The Hunan Diner, the local Chinese eatery, advertises a "Redskins Lounge."

Sightseeing motorists driving either side of the lower Potomac today will appreciate why early residents preferred river travel. Inlets and broad tidal creeks penetrate deeply into Virginia and Maryland, offering handy water access to points inland and necessitating the setting of roads far back from the waterfront.

It was along one of these inlets, Popes Creek in Virginia, that George Washington first saw light. He was born during the chilly Potomac winter of 1732, in February — "a formidable month in which to make an

Top photos — The lower Potomac divided Catholic Maryland and Protestant Virginia. Colonial Marylanders were inspired by the beautiful stained glass of Trinity Church in St. Marys City.

Above — Virginians worshipped in the Anglican St. Stephens Parish originally formed in 1653 as Chickacone Parish.

Top — Cliffs along the banks of the Potomac on the Virginia side near Stratford Hall.

Left — Colonial Beach in Virginia was a popular resort for the Washington, D.C., corwd in years past. (Photo courtesy Virginia State Library and Archives)

Below — Aerial view of Colonial Beach, which still draws visitors with its fishing piers, waterfront attractions, and restaurants.

appearance on this earth," as he later opined. Popes Creek Plantation is administered today as a national monument by the National Park Service. The house of Washington's birth no longer stands, but the surrounding farm has been extensively restored, much of it now farmed as a living history site.

Popes Creek was a modest establishment by the standards of the Lees and some other Westmoreland County neighbors, for the Washingtons were then on the rise rather than at the top of society. Their plantation occupies a site of deep tranquility, suffused by the special light of woods and water. It was a fitting site for the birthplace of the father of the country, and it was here that he began a lifelong relationship with the adjoining Potomac.

The major tributaries flow in from the Maryland side along this final stretch of the Potomac. Port Tobacco River flows down from historic Port Tobacco town, whose site was noted on Captain John Smith's map of 1608. The Wicomico River and Wicomico Bay empty into the Potomac next, then St. Clements Creek by way of St. Clements Bay, and after that Breton Bay and St. Marys River. St. Marys is the last of the tributaries, flowing in from the north just before the Maryland shore filigrees down to a ragged point between the Chesapeake Bay and the Potomac River.

Although relatively few, river islands play their part in the history and ecology of the tidal Potomac. St. Clements Island, lying just off Colton's Point at the mouth of St. Clements Bay, was the first landing place of the Maryland settlers and the site of the first Roman Catholic mass to be celebrated in British North America. St. George Island, lying at the mouth of St. Marys River, is known today for its restaurants and as a winter gathering point for great cormorants. St. George may be reached by highway bridge, as may smaller Cobb Island upstream, while St. Clements remains true to its historic character as a part of the water world of the Potomac, accessible only by boat.

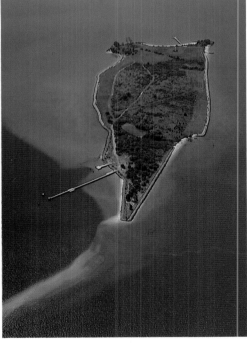

Top — Aerial view of Leonardtown, county seat of St. Marys County, Maryland, with Breton Bay in the background.

St. Clements Island in the Potomac, in 1634 the first landing site of Maryland's founders, is now a state park.

Above — Scenes from times past show the abundance of fish caught in the lower Potomac. (Photos courtesy Virginia State Library and Archives)

Facing page — Today the banks of the lower Potomac offer marinas, beaches and fine homes, reflecting recreational use of the river.

The Potomac River pours itself into the choppy waters of the Chesapeake Bay at Point Lookout. This pennisula guarding the only naval approach to America's capital city has been occupied by a succession of military facilities, although earlier vigilance has long since been relaxed. A dilapidated Navy tracking station now straddles the point, with a squat lighthouse inside the military compound. Adjoining Point Comfort State Park is more characteristic of the peaceable nature of the place today. The park is a favorite fishing spot, with the Potomac side of the point crowded with fishermen on weekends throughout much of the year. Point Comfort State Park is excellent birdwatching territory, especially as migratory flocks make their way along the flyways from fall to spring.

The nearby Point Lookout Confederate Cemetery marks a darker time, the grimmest period of local history. Here are buried the remains of nearly 3,400 Confederate prisoners of war who perished at the Camp Hoffman federal prison compound. The unfortunate men incarcerated at Camp Hoffman died at an average rate of dozens daily from March 1864 through June 1865. Their memorial is a striking obelisk, bearing each man's name and an inscription stating that it was "erected by the United States to mark the burial places of Confederate soldiers and sailors." Supposedly this lonely stone shaft is the only federal monument to the Southern cause.

Crossing the broad mouth of the Potomac, more than 11 watery miles from Point Lookout to Smith Point, brings one back to Virginia, to Northumberland County, the mother county of the Northern Neck. Reedsville is the big town here, a community with a surprising number of Victorian mansions left over from fishing industry fortunes of earlier times. Reedsville's treasures were drawn largely from salt water, for nearby Smith Point marks not only an end to the land but a mingling of waters, the place where the Potomac River merges itself into the rich estuary of the Chesapeake Bay.

*Fields of yellow grace the banks
of the Potomac on the Virginia
side, close to where the river
empties in the Chesapeake Bay.*

*Below — A farmhouse stands like
an island among the fields
bordering the Potomac.*

Standing here and looking out toward the Chesapeake, the visitor stands finally with his back to all of the Potomac watershed, to the hundreds of miles of fast-moving and slow-moving waters, to mountain and piedmont, to dozens of small towns and one huge metropolis, and to a considerable chunk of the American story.

This is low country. Virginia's Northern Neck and the corresponding countryside on the Maryland shore are not exactly flat, but parts lie near enough to sea level that if the visitor comes from the mountainous upper Potomac region — say from the highlands of Pendleton County, West Virginia, or Garrett County, Maryland — he may think the whole place in danger of submersion during the torential rainstorms which sometimes whip in from the bayside. It isn't, actually, for this tenacious land has withstood the worst of the weather since Captain Smith's visit of 1608 and for untold ages before that. And the upland visitor may be humbled by this long sweep of time itself, by a recorded history a century and more older than his. It all goes to show the difference in the upper and lower river and the broad diversity of the Potomac watershed.

But if this visitor has made his trip downstream by riverside — from the North Branch to the South Branch with its separate South and North forks, past the Savage River, the Shenandoah, the Anacostia and the many other Potomac tributaries, through Westernport, Cumberland, Harpers Ferry, Shepherdstown, Washington and Alexandria, and by the countless smaller towns bearing names as wonderful as Point of Rocks, Brandywine, Sleepy Creek and Falling Waters — he will recognize the thread of continuity to be the flowing water itself, the ancient stream which has created valley, plains, gaps and passes and allowed for the human and natural communities which occupy these places.

Father Andrew White considered the river in its lower stretches greater than England's greatest, Thomas Jefferson thought a single view of the valley worth a trip across the ocean, and illustrator Porte Crayon found as many scenic wonders on the North Fork as in a world tour. They exaggerated, no doubt. To decide how much you will have to come see for yourself, just as they intended.

The Potomac which starts as fledgling mountain streams in the high country of West Virginia and Virginia ends as a wide tidal river in the lowlands of Maryland and Virginia.

Photographer's Afterword

A river presents a definite area to photograph. There is a beginning and an end, and it never strays from its banks. But that doesn't mean it's easy. Any river is challenging in the variety of sites it offers and in the multiplicity of human and natural environments along its banks.

All the more so for the Potomac. This is an especially diverse river system, from the tumbling mountain tributaries, which seem as new as yesterday and which one can jump across in many places, to the ponderous tidal river touched with the weight of centuries of history and miles wide in most places.

Much has been written about the Potomac and many photographs taken, but there have been surprisingly few pictorial books on the whole river. As far as I know, there has been nothing of the sort of words-and-pictures biography that Ken Sullivan and I decided to undertake back in 1991. You have the report of Ken's travels in the preceding pages. Let me offer some brief impressions of my own, some favorite memories from the past few years of floating, driving and flying up and down the Potomac Valley.

It is difficult to know just what to include and what to exclude.

For example, I remember setting up my camera several times at the spring that begins the South Branch on the John Hevener farm in Highland County, Virginia. As it happens, that spring also serves a watering trough in Hevener's meadow, and each time I appeared a large Hevener bull invited me in no uncertain terms to leave.

And each time I obliged, dragging camera gear back over the split rail fence, preserving my hide if not my dignity.

Then there was a confrontation of a more modern sort, though with less hostile intent. This happened down at the other end of the river, as John Green and I flew in a single-engine Cessna to take aerial photographs. John landed outside the Patuxent River Naval Air Station, which encompasses the broad low country where the Potomac empties into the Chesapeake Bay, and called to ask permission to fly within this highly restricted area.

The military authorities agreed — provided their FA-18 jet fighters could use us as targets. They promised that their aviators would only "lock in" with their radar, and release no missiles. I'm here to report that the Navy guys kept their end of the bargain, as did we.

And I recall one summer night climbing Maryland Heights with flashlights to wait on the cliffs for the sun to rise over Harpers Ferry. That produced the photograph you see on pages 70 and 71.

Finally, there was the eerie, misty morning at Burnside Bridge at Antietam National Battlefield, the site of the bloodiest day's fighting of the Civil War. As I set up my camera and tripod I was startled to hear rapid, ghostly voices which seemed to emanate from the ground and lasted for perhaps 30 seconds.

I can't explain that and won't try to, but it was very much a part of what made this book project a memorable one.

Acknowledgments

I would like to recognize and express my appreciation to some special people who helped me on this book.

First, my very supportive and loving family, Teresa and Lucia Katherine, and my mother and father, Arnie and Kate, have always been a source of encouragement. Julie and Stephen Seaman, who reside outside Washington, put me up while I was in that area — and Julie sent me off in the mornings with fresh-baked, homemade muffins.

John Green's flying skills always seemed to put me in the right position for an aerial photograph. Ida Smookler is a wonderful lady whose love for the Potomac could always find me someone, somewhere, who had information on any section of the river.

My Congressman, Robert Wise of West Virginia, graciously supplied information from government sources when requested. Gordon Gay, Chief Interpreter for the Chesapeake & Ohio Canal National Historic Park, provided old photographs and information on the park. Carolyn S. Parsons of the Virginia State Library and Archives researched and found old black-and-white photos of the lower portion of the Potomac.

Collaborating with writer Ken Sullivan was a rewarding endeavor. Working for the most part independently of one another, we seem to have intuitively matched text and photographs, and we share an enthusiasm for the river.

As Ken and I wrapped up our fieldwork and the project began to take final shape, I turned the basic layout over to two very talented people in the graphic arts business, Lance Bell and Kathie Smith of AAD-INC. (Advertising Art Design Inc.), of Cumberland, Maryland, to refine the looks and produce finished artwork for this publication. What better company than one in that historic old town on the banks of the Potomac to give the book its final face?

— Arnout Hyde, Jr.

Many friends contributed to this book, as tributaries contribute to the Potomac River. This is Opequon Creek in West Virginia, blanketed in winter.

This book is dedicated to my loving wife, Teresa, who journeyed with me on trips up and down the Potomac.